GREAT MINDS® WIT & WISDOM

# Grade 3 Module 2
## Outer Space

*Student Edition*

**GREAT MINDS**

Great Minds® is the creator of *Eureka Math*®,
*Wit & Wisdom*®, *Alexandria Plan*™, and *PhD Science*®.

Published by Great Minds PBC
greatminds.org

© 2023 Great Minds PBC. All rights reserved. No part of this work may be reproduced or used in any form or by any means—graphic, electronic, or mechanical, including photocopying or information storage and retrieval systems—without written permission from the copyright holder.

Printed in the USA

A-Print

1 2 3 4 5 6 7 8 9 10 QDG 27 26 25 24 23

979-8-88588-741-0

# Student Edition

## GRADE 3 MODULE 2

### Lesson Handouts

Handout 1A: Speaking and Listening Development and Process Rubric

Handout 1B: Speaking and Listening Process Checklist

Handout 1C: Reading Log

Handout 2A: "Galileo's Starry Night"

Handout 2B: Speaking and Listening Process Checklist

Handout 2C: Developing a Topic

Handout 2D: Fluency Homework

Handout 3A: Describe Your Knowledge "To a TEE" Writing Planner

Handout 5A: Describe Your Knowledge "To a TEE" Writing Planner

Handout 6A: Describe Your Knowledge "To a TEE" Writing Planner

Handout 7A: Script Passages from *Starry Messenger: Galileo Galilei*

Handout 7B: Using Illustrations and Words in *Starry Messenger: Galileo Galilei*

Handout 7C: Speaking and Listening Process Checklist

Handout 7D: Essay Organization

Handout 7E: Fluency Homework

Handout 9A: Frayer Model

Handout 10A: Socratic Seminar Participation Guidelines

Handout 10B: Socratic Seminar Self-Assessment

Handout 10C: Conclusion Paragraph Writing Checklist

Handout 11A: Speaking and Listening Process Checklist

Handout 11B: Describe Your Knowledge "To a Tee" Writing Planner

Handout 11C: Deconstructing Compound Sentences

Handout 12A: Focusing Question Task 1 Checklist

Handout 12B: Using Compound Sentences

Handout 13A: Fluency Homework

Handout 14A: Apollo 11 Events in *Moonshot*

Handout 16A: Identifying Points of View

Handout 16B: Tableau Checklist

Handout 17A: Analyzing Repetition

Handout 17B: Writing Planner

Handout 18A: "Apollo 11: The *Eagle* Has Landed"

Handout 19A: Model Opinion Paragraph

Handout 19B: Fluency Homework

Handout 19C: Frayer Model

Handout 20A: Apollo 11 Events in *One Giant Leap*

Handout 21A: Nonliteral Language in *One Giant Leap*

Handout 23A: "We Choose the Moon," from a speech by President John F. Kennedy

Handout 24A: Socratic Seminar Self-Assessment

Handout 24B: Taking Apart "We Choose the Moon"

Handout 25A: Comparing and Contrasting Texts

Handout 25B: Writing Planner

Handout 26A: Focusing Question Task 2 Checklist

Handout 27A: Story Map

Handout 27B: Fluency Homework

Handout 27C: Morpheme Matrix

Handout 30A: "Pegasus and Perseus" and "Pegasus and Bellerophon"

Handout 30B: Recounting a Myth

Handout 30C: Speaking and Listening Process Checklist

Handout 31A: Organizer for Research Notes

Handout 32A: Socratic Seminar Self-Assessment

Handout 32B: Vocabulary Study Guide

Handout 33A: Writing Planner

Handout 34A: Focusing Question Task 3 Checklist

Handout 34B: Making Revisions

Handout 35A: Writing Planner

Handout 36A: End-of-Module Task Checklist

Volume of Reading Reflection Questions

*Wit & Wisdom* Family Tip Sheet

# Name

# Handout 1A: Speaking and Listening Development and Process Rubric

**Directions:** Use the rubric on the following page to set goals and assess speaking and listening processes in Module 2.

# Grade 3 Speaking and Listening Development and Process Rubric

| | 4 (Exceeds Expectations) | 3 (Meets Expectations) | 2 (Partially Meets Expectations) | 1 (Does Not Yet Meet Expectations) |
|---|---|---|---|---|
| **Development** | • Reports thoroughly on topics and texts using relevant and descriptive details.<br>• Recounts stories and experiences with appropriate facts and relevant details.<br>• Anticipates and provides clarification when speaking.<br>• Prepares thoroughly in advance for discussions and draws extensively on that preparation. | • Reports on topics and texts using relevant and descriptive details.<br>• Recounts stories and experiences with appropriate facts and relevant details.<br>• Provides clarification when requested.<br>• Prepares in advance for discussions. | • Reports on topics and texts using details.<br>• Recounts stories and experiences with some facts and details.<br>• Says more when requested.<br>• Reads text for discussions. | • Does not yet report on topics and texts using details.<br>• Does not recount stories and experiences.<br>• Does not respond to requests.<br>• Does not prepare for discussions. |
| **Process** | • Alternates speaking and listening in conversations through multiple exchanges.<br>• Follows all agreed-upon rules for conversations.<br>• Links comments to comments of others effectively.<br>• Agrees and disagrees respectfully and strategically.<br>• Contributions indicate curiosity.<br>• Creates expressive and engaging audio recordings of fluently read stories or poems. | • Speaks in conversations through multiple exchanges.<br>• Follows most agreed-upon rules for conversations.<br>• Links comments to comments of others.<br>• Agrees and disagrees respectfully.<br>• Contributions indicate engagement.<br>• Creates engaging audio recordings of fluently read stories or poems. | • Speaks in conversations.<br>• Follows some agreed-upon rules for conversations.<br>• Sometimes links comments to comments of others.<br>• Indicates agreement and/or disagreement.<br>• Contributions indicate compliance.<br>• Creates audio recordings of stories or poems. | • Does not yet speak in conversations.<br>• Follows few, if any, agreed-upon rules for conversations.<br>• Rarely, if ever, links comments to comments of others.<br>• Does not yet indicate agreement or disagreement.<br>• Contributions do not yet indicate compliance.<br>• Does not yet create audio recordings of stories or poems. |
| **Listening** | • Facial expressions and body language demonstrate curiosity.<br>• Can repeat back what is heard in sequence from memory.<br>• Listens actively and cues the speaker with gestures and facial expressions. | • Eye contact and body language demonstrate attention.<br>• Can repeat back what is heard in sequence.<br>• Cues the speaker with gestures and/or facial expressions. | • Tracks speakers.<br>• Can repeat back what is heard.<br>• Sometimes gives the speaker cues. | • Sometimes tracks speakers.<br>• Does not yet repeat back what is heard.<br>• Does not yet give the speaker cues. |

# Name

# Handout 1B: Speaking and Listening Process Checklist

**Directions:** Use the checklist below to monitor how well you used your speaking and listening skills. Then ask a classmate to evaluate how well you used the skills. Your teacher will complete the third column, based on what they observe.

| Grade 3 Speaking and Listening Process Checklist | | | |
|---|---|---|---|
| | Self +/ Δ | Peer +/ Δ | Teacher +/ Δ |
| I took turns speaking and listening. | | | |
| I followed all the rules for working in a small group. | | | |
| I linked my comments to comments from other people. | | | |
| I agreed and disagreed respectfully. | | | |
| • I used a polite tone of voice throughout the discussion. | | | |
| • I used a sentence stem to help me agree or disagree respectfully. | | | |

| | | | |
|---|---|---|---|
| • I used a nonverbal cue to show that I agreed or disagreed with a speaker. | | | |
| I explained my thinking in light of our discussion. | | | |
| I used appropriate facts and details to report on a topic or text. | | | |
| I spoke clearly at an understandable pace. | | | |
| My comments showed that I am curious about what we are learning. | | | |
| My comments showed that I can recount what others say. | | | |

# Name

# Handout 1C: Reading Log

**Directions:** Track your daily reading by recording the date, genre, title and author, and how many pages you read.

| Date Started | Literature (L) or Informational (I) Text | Title and Author | Pages Read |
|---|---|---|---|
|  |  |  |  |
|  |  |  |  |
|  |  |  |  |
|  |  |  |  |
|  |  |  |  |
|  |  |  |  |
|  |  |  |  |
|  |  |  |  |
|  |  |  |  |
|  |  |  |  |

# Handout 2A: "Galileo's Starry Night"

**Directions:** Read the text below, annotating for new or confusing words.

1. On a warm June evening in 1609, Galileo Galilei, a forty-five-year-old Italian mathematics teacher and father of three, listened as a friend described the latest invention to hit Europe: a long tube containing two glass lenses, called a spyglass.

2. "It makes faraway things appear close! We could use one of those here in Italy," the friend said. "Perhaps you could try to build one, if you're interested."

3. Was he ever! Galileo loved trying to figure out how the world and the things in it worked. That very night he leaped into the project with gusto. In a short time, he not only figured out how to construct a spyglass, he improved upon the existing model as well.

4. When he later presented his device to the rulers of Venice, they marveled at how far it could see. The spyglass would be quite useful for spotting distant enemies, making it hard for anyone to launch a sneak attack!

5. Galileo wasn't satisfied, however, and he kept fiddling with his "telescope," as his fellow mathematician friend Giovanni Demisiani had called it (the word means "far-looker"). He tried new adjustments and worked at grinding better lenses. Within a few months, he had a telescope that was three times more powerful than his first.

6. By now, autumn had arrived, and evenings darkened early. One night as the moon rose, Galileo pointed his telescope toward the sky. If it could see far on Earth, why not into the heavens as well? Who knew what the moon might look like close up?

7. What Galileo saw astonished him. The moon was not perfectly smooth, as it appeared to the naked eye. It was a bumpy moon. Its edges had "ridges of darkness" and "pips of lights," and it was covered with what looked like craters, mountains, and valleys. Entranced by these unexpected details, Galileo drew picture after picture of what he saw through the telescope.

8. A craggy moon wasn't all that he discovered. Galileo could now see that the Milky Way, seemingly a bright cloud across the sky, was in fact made of millions of stars. He also noticed that while fixed stars of constellations looked like twinkling lights, the "wandering stars," or planets, seemed to be solid spheres—like the moon.

9. All through that December, Galileo peered into the night sky at what had never been seen before. Sometimes his hands shook with the cold. The chilled lens of his telescope fogged up whenever he put his eye near the glass, and he had to keep wiping it clear.

# Name

10  On January 7, 1610, Galileo focused his gaze on Jupiter. He noticed three bright stars beside it and drew a sketch of them. The next night he looked again. The three stars had scooted to new positions! How odd, he thought. The following night, Galileo saw only two stars. What was going on? A few nights later he saw four. Galileo kept watching and recording his observations until he concluded that these dots were neither stars nor planets—they were little moons, circling Jupiter!

11  Galileo wrote down his observations and thoughts in a book called *The Starry Messenger*. The book immediately sold out. People were very excited—and troubled—by his discoveries.

12  Little moons circling not Earth, but Jupiter? Our own moon a bumpy one? Sightings like these could change how people thought about the universe. Some skeptics chose not to look through the new telescopes; others refused to believe what they saw. They insisted that Galileo put specks in his telescopes to trick people.

13  Feverishly, Galileo built more telescopes, hoping to make the truth visible to everyone. But what kind of truth was this? Could you really trust a telescope? And what did it all mean?

14  These early telescopes weren't perfect, but what they showed was true enough: the heavens were not "flawless," nor did they revolve around the earth, as many believed. Instead, it looked like the many planets, including Earth, revolved around the sun.

15. Those who lived in the 1600s were not quite ready for this scientific breakthrough. At the time, many people passionately believed Earth should be at the center of the universe. Galileo was ordered to stop writing about his observations and was imprisoned in his house. He was put on trial, and his books were banned for two hundred years.

16. However, people had already begun to see what they had not been able to see before, and they started to ask questions. While some refused to let go of their old ideas, new and marvelous mysteries and discoveries awaited those who did.

# Name

# Handout 2B: Speaking and Listening Process Checklist

**Directions:** Use the checklist below to monitor how well you used your speaking and listening skills. Then ask a classmate to evaluate how well you used the skills. Your teacher will complete the third column, based on what they observe.

| Grade 3 Speaking and Listening Process Checklist | Self +/ Δ | Peer +/ Δ | Teacher +/ Δ |
|---|---|---|---|
| I took turns speaking and listening. | | | |
| I followed all the rules for working in a small group. | | | |
| I linked my comments to comments from other people. | | | |

| | | | |
|---|---|---|---|
| I agreed and disagreed respectfully. | | | |
| • I used a polite tone of voice throughout the discussion. | | | |
| • I used a sentence stem to help me agree or disagree respectfully. | | | |
| • I used a nonverbal cue to show that I agreed or disagreed with a speaker. | | | |
| I explained my thinking in light of our discussion. | | | |
| I used appropriate facts and details to report on a topic or text. | | | |
| I spoke clearly at an understandable pace. | | | |
| My comments showed that I am curious about what we are learning. | | | |
| My comments showed that I can recount what others say. | | | |

# Handout 2C: Developing a Topic

**Directions:** After reading "Galileo's Starry Night," by Kelly Terwilliger, work with your group to examine how the author develops the topic by sorting the facts, definitions, and details next to the topic they explain.

| Topic | Fact | Definition | Detail |
|---|---|---|---|
| spyglass | | | |
| telescope | | | |
| moon | | | |
| Jupiter | | | |

---

three bright stars beside it

He tried new adjustments and worked at grinding better lenses.

a long tube containing two glass lenses

he had a telescope that was three times more powerful than his first

means "far-looker"

dots were neither stars nor planets—they were little moons, circling Jupiter

not perfectly smooth

useful for spotting distant enemies

covered with what looked like craters, mountains, and valleys

makes faraway things appear close

# Name

# Handout 3A: Describe Your Knowledge "To a TEE" Writing Planner

**Directions:** Read the prompt below, and choose two pieces of supporting evidence. Identify the type of evidence by circling Fact, Definition, or Detail. Elaborate by explaining how each piece of evidence supports the topic sentence.

Prompt: Write a paragraph explaining why Galileo is an important astronomer. Remember to use facts, definitions, and details from *Starry Messenger: Galileo Galilei* to develop your paragraph.

| | | | |
|---|---|---|---|
| **T** | Topic Statement | | Galileo Galilei is an important astronomer because of his many discoveries. |
| **E** | Evidence | Fact<br>Definition<br>Detail | |
| **E** | | | |
| **E** | | Fact<br>Definition<br>Detail | For these reasons, Galileo is an important astronomer. |
| **E** | | | |
| **C** | | | |

When you are finished planning, write the paragraph in complete sentences. Use the Painted Essay® strategy to check that you have described your knowledge "to a TEE."

Paragraph:

# Name

# Handout 5A: Describe Your Knowledge "To a TEE" Writing Planner

**Directions:** Choose two pieces of supporting evidence. Identify the type of evidence by circling Fact, Definition, or Detail. Elaborate by explaining how each piece of evidence supports the topic sentence.

Prompt: Explain what happened when Galileo went against tradition. Use facts, definitions, and details to develop the paragraph.

| | | | |
|---|---|---|---|
| **T** | Topic Statement | | A long time ago people followed tradition and believed the earth was the center of the universe. |
| **E** | Evidence | Fact<br>Definition<br>Detail | |
| **E** | | | |
| **E** | | Fact<br>Definition<br>Detail | |
| **E** | | | |
| **C** | | | The church locked Galileo in his house for the rest of his life, but his ideas lived on. |

When you are finished planning, write the paragraph in complete sentences. Use the Painted Essay® strategy to check that you have described your knowledge "to a TEE."

Paragraph:

_____
_____
_____
_____
_____
_____
_____
_____
_____
_____
_____

# Name

# Handout 6A: Describe Your Knowledge "To a TEE" Writing Planner

**Directions:** Use the introduction below, and focus your attention on well-developed body paragraphs. The last sentence in the introduction is a sentence frame to preview your two supporting reasons.

Prompt: Page 26 of *Starry Messenger* says, "everyone could see that the stars had left his eyes." Write an essay explaining why the stars left Galileo's eyes. Use facts, definitions, and details to develop the topic.

# Introductory Paragraph

In *Starry Messenger*, by Peter Sís, the story of Galileo's birth begins with an illustration of babies. Each baby is wrapped in a blanket that shows what they would become as an adult. Galileo is wrapped in a blanket with pictures of stars, and the text says, "a little boy was born with stars in his eyes" [8]. Later in the story, on page [28], it says, "everyone could see that the stars had left his eyes." The stars left Galileo's eyes because _____ and because _____.

## Body Paragraph 1

| | | | |
|---|---|---|---|
| T | Topic Statement | | |
| E | Evidence | Fact Definition Detail | |
| E | Elaboration | | |

## Body Paragraph 2

| | | | |
|---|---|---|---|
| T | Topic Statement | | |
| E | Evidence | Fact Definition Detail | |
| E | Elaboration | | |

# Name

# Handout 7A: Script Passages from *Starry Messenger: Galileo Galilei*

**Directions:** If you have trouble reading the script passages on the pages of *Starry Messenger*, use the typed versions below.

## Page [3]

"God fixed the earth upon its foundation, not to be moved for ever." —Psalms

## Page [6]

Italy was a quilt of city-states, each with its own laws and government. A common religion, the Catholic faith, was one thing they all shared, and the Church was a powerful influence.

## Page [8]

Galileo Galilei
born February 15, 1564

Father: Vincennio Galilei, cloth merchant,
Accomplished musician, and mathematician.

William Shakespeare was also born in 1564.
Michelangelo died in that same year.

"Be not afraid of greatness: some are born great, some achieve greatness, and some have greatness thrust upon them." — William Shakespeare, *Twelfth Night* (II, v. 159)

## Page [10]

Until the age of eleven, Galileo was taught at home by his father. Then he was sent to the Benedictine Monastery of Santa Maria di Vallombrosa where he studied Latin, Greek, religion and music.

In Galileo's time, homes and cities were often beautiful, but life was difficult and luxuries few. Light came from candles or oil lamps. There was no refrigeration. The streets were open sewers. Disease was common, and thousands died from typhus and from the bubonic plague.

## Page [12]

1581
Entered the University of Pisa. Was an argumentative student and questioned the teachings of Aristotle. Left the university to study mathematics and physics on his own. Became Professor of Mathematics at the University of Pisa when he was just twenty-five years old.

1592. Became Professor of Mathematics at the University of Padua. Did experiments proving Aristotle wrong. Discovered the Law of Falling Objects by showing that two balls of unequal weight fall at the same speed.

# Name

The Law of Floating Objects
1611

The Law of Falling Objects
1604

The Law of the Pendulum
1583

Invented and perfected instruments that brought new accuracy to science: a hydrostatic balance, the first practical thermometer, a geometric and military compass, a compound microscope, and the first astronomical telescope.

Page [14]

"A report reached my ears that a certain Fleming had constructed a spyglass ... Upon hearing the news, I set myself to thinking about the problem ... Finally, sparing neither labor nor expense, I succeeded in constructing for myself so excellent an instrument that objects seen by means of it appeared nearly one thousand times larger and over thirty times closer than when regarded with our natural vision." (The word *telescope* was coined two years later, in 1611.)

# Page [16]

## *The Starry Messenger*

Revealing great, unusual and remarkable spectacles
opening those to the consideration of every man, and
especially of philosophers and astronomers,
as observed by Galileo Galilei
Gentleman of Florence
Professor of Mathematics in the
University of Padua
With the Aid of a
Spyglass
Lately invented by him,
In the surface of the Moon, in innumerable
Fixed Stars, in Nebulae, and above all
in FOUR PLANETS
swiftly revolving about Jupiter at
differing distances and periods,
and known to no one before the
Author recently perceived them
and decided that they should
be named
THE MEDICEAN STARS
Venice
1610

# Name

## pages [16–17]

|  | There are astronomical arguments derived from many things in my new celestial discoveries that plainly confute the Ptolemaic system while admirably agreeing with and confirming the contrary hypothesis. |  |
|---|---|---|
| It is a beautiful thing and most gratifying to the sight to behold the body of the moon. |  | Covered everywhere, just like the earth's surface. |
| The moon is not robed in a smooth and polished surface but is in fact rough and uneven. |  | With huge prominences deep valleys, and chasms. |
|  | I have observed the nature and material of the Milky Way. With the aid of the telescope this has been scrutinized so directly and with such regular certainty that all the aspects which have vexed philosophers through so many ages have been resolved, and we are at last freed from wordy debates about it. The galaxy is, in fact, nothing but a congeries of innumerable stars grouped together in clusters. |  |

## Page [18]

"[I] know rather what sunspots are not than what they really are, it being much harder for me to discover the truth than to refute what is false."

"I have no doubt whatsoever that they are real objects and not mere appearances or illusions of the eye or of the lenses of the telescope."

"I liken the sunspots to clouds or smokes."

"I shall now describe the method of drawing the spots with complete accuracy ... Direct the telescope upon the sun. ... Expose a flat white sheet of paper about a foot from the concave lens ... With a pen one may mark out the spots in their right sizes, shapes, and positions."

## Page [25]

"I hold the sun to be situated motionless in the center of the revolution of the celestial orbs while the earth rotates on its own axis and revolves around the sun."

## Page [26]

"I do not feel obliged to believe that the same God who has endowed us with senses, reason, and intellect has intended to forgo their use. ... He would not require us to deny sense and reason in physical matters which are set before our eyes and minds by direct experience or necessary demonstrations."

"If they [the ancient philosophers] had seen what we see, they would have judged as we judge."

# Name

"Why should I believe blindly and stupidly what I wish to believe, and subject the freedom of my intellect to someone else who is just as liable to error as I am?"

Page [28]

The Inquisition found Galileo guilty of heresy.

"Namely for having held and believed a doctrine which is false and contrary to the divine and Holy Scripture, that the sun is the center of the world and does not move from east to west, and the earth moves and is not the center of the world and that one may hold and defend as probable an opinion after it has been declared and defined contrary to the Holy Scripture."

June 1633 ROME

Page [30]

"In the sciences the authority of thousands of opinions is not worth as much as one tiny spark of reason in an individual man."

"I think that in discussion of physical problems (Nature) we ought to begin not from the authority of scriptural passages, but from sense-experiences and necessary demonstrations."

"With regard to matters requiring thought: the less people know and understand about them, the more positively they attempt to argue concerning them."

**Page [32]**

June 1633—Galileo sentenced
January 8, 1642—Galileo dies
October 18, 1989—Galileo spacecraft launched
October 31, 1991—Galileo pardoned

---

Sís, Peter. *Starry Messenger: Galileo Galilei*. Square Fish, 2000.

# Name

# Handout 7B: Using Illustrations and Words in *Starry Messenger: Galileo Galilei*

**Directions:**

1. Examine the text, illustrations, and passage(s) in script on the assigned pages.

2. Determine the main idea of the passage, and record it in the appropriate box.

3. Record details in the text, illustrations, and passages in script that support the main idea.

4. Meet with other groups to discuss the pages you did not analyze and complete the table. As a group, identify the main idea of pages [12–17], and write a sentence expressing the main idea below this chart.

Assigned pages: _____

| Main idea: | |
|---|---|
| Evidence from the text that supports the main idea: | |
| Evidence from the illustration(s) that supports the main idea: | |
| Evidence from the script that supports the main idea: | |

# Name

# Handout 7C: Speaking and Listening Process Checklist

**Directions:** Use the checklist below to monitor how well you used your speaking and listening skills. Then ask a classmate to evaluate how well you used the skills. Your teacher will complete the third column, based on what they observe.

| Grade 3 Speaking and Listening Process Checklist | | | |
|---|---|---|---|
|  | Self +/ Δ | Peer +/ Δ | Teacher +/ Δ |
| I took turns speaking and listening. | | | |
| I followed all the rules for working in a small group. | | | |
| I linked my comments to comments from other people. | | | |
| I agreed and disagreed respectfully. | | | |

| | | | |
|---|---|---|---|
| • I used a polite tone of voice throughout the discussion. | | | |
| • I used a sentence stem to help me agree or disagree respectfully. | | | |
| • I used a nonverbal cue to show that I agreed or disagreed with a speaker. | | | |
| I explained my thinking in light of our discussion. | | | |
| I used appropriate facts and details to report on a topic or text. | | | |
| I spoke clearly at an understandable pace. | | | |
| My comments showed that I am curious about what we are learning. | | | |
| My comments showed that I can recount what others say. | | | |

# Name

# Handout 7D: Essay Organization

**Directions:** Read each of the paragraphs below, and then number and label each paragraph correctly. Label each paragraph as either an introduction (I), a body paragraph (B), or a conclusion (C).

| Paragraph Order | Type of Paragraph: (introduction, body, conclusion) | Paragraph |
|---|---|---|
|  |  | Pages [16] and [17] show how Galileo used the telescope to observe the moon. It says, "Night after night, he gazed through his telescope and wrote down everything he observed." The center picture shows Galileo looking at the sky through his telescope. The small pictures show what he saw through the telescope. The captions in script explain what Galileo saw. He says the moon is "not smooth and polished." The text, illustrations, and text features help the reader to understand Galileo's new observations about the moon. |

|  |  | Peter Sís tells the story of Galileo Galilei in *Starry Messenger*. Peter Sís uses text features, illustrations, and text to explain why Galileo was so famous. Galileo was an astronomer who used his telescope to discover new things about the moon and the sun. He did not just follow tradition. He tried to observe the sky and learn new things. |
|---|---|---|
|  |  | *Starry Messenger* is very interesting. The book uses text, illustrations, and text features to tell about Galileo Galilei's discoveries. |
|  |  | The book also says that Galileo discovered new things about the sun. On page [18], it says, "Galileo was amazed by what he could see with his telescope." A picture on pages [18–19] shows the sun with sun spots. The script says Galileo used his telescope to learn about sun spots and then sketched them. These help the reader to understand the sun better. |

# Name _____

# Handout 7E: Fluency Homework

**Directions:**

1. Day 1: Read the text carefully, and annotate to help you read fluently.

2. Each day:
   a. Practice reading the text aloud three to five times.
   b. Evaluate your progress by placing a √+, √, or √- in the appropriate, unshaded box.
   c. Ask someone (adult or peer) to listen and to evaluate your reading.

3. Last day: Fill out the Self-reflection section at the end.

## Starry Messenger

### by Peter Sís

Then one day Galileo heard about a new instrument for seeing things far, far away. He figured out how it worked and made one for himself. Then he turned it to the sky.

Night after night, he gazed through his telescope and wrote down everything he observed. Then he published his observations in a book which he called *The Starry Messenger*.

Galileo was amazed by what he could see with his telescope.

Soon Galileo was famous. More and more people celebrated the stars, and they celebrated Galileo and his discoveries with statues and parades and spectacular events.

Sís, Peter. *Starry Messenger: Galileo Galilei*. Square Fish, 2000, pp. [14–18, 23].

# Name

| Student Performance Checklist | Day 1 You | Day 1 Listener* | Day 2 You | Day 2 Listener* | Day 3 You | Day 3 Listener* | Day 4 You | Day 4 Listener* |
|---|---|---|---|---|---|---|---|---|
| Accurately read the passage three to five times. | | | | | | | | |
| Read with appropriate phrasing and pausing. | ▓ | | | | | | | |
| Read with appropriate expression. | ▓ | | ▓ | | | | | |
| Read articulately at a good pace and an audible volume. | ▓ | | ▓ | | ▓ | | | |

*Adult or peer

**Self-reflection:** What choices did you make when deciding how to read this passage, and why? What would you like to improve on or try to do differently next time? (Thoughtfully answer these questions on the back of this paper.)

# Name

# Handout 9A: Frayer Model

**Directions:** Using a dictionary, chart the multiple meanings of the word *influence*, and complete the Frayer Model for the word with definitions, characteristics, examples, and nonexamples.

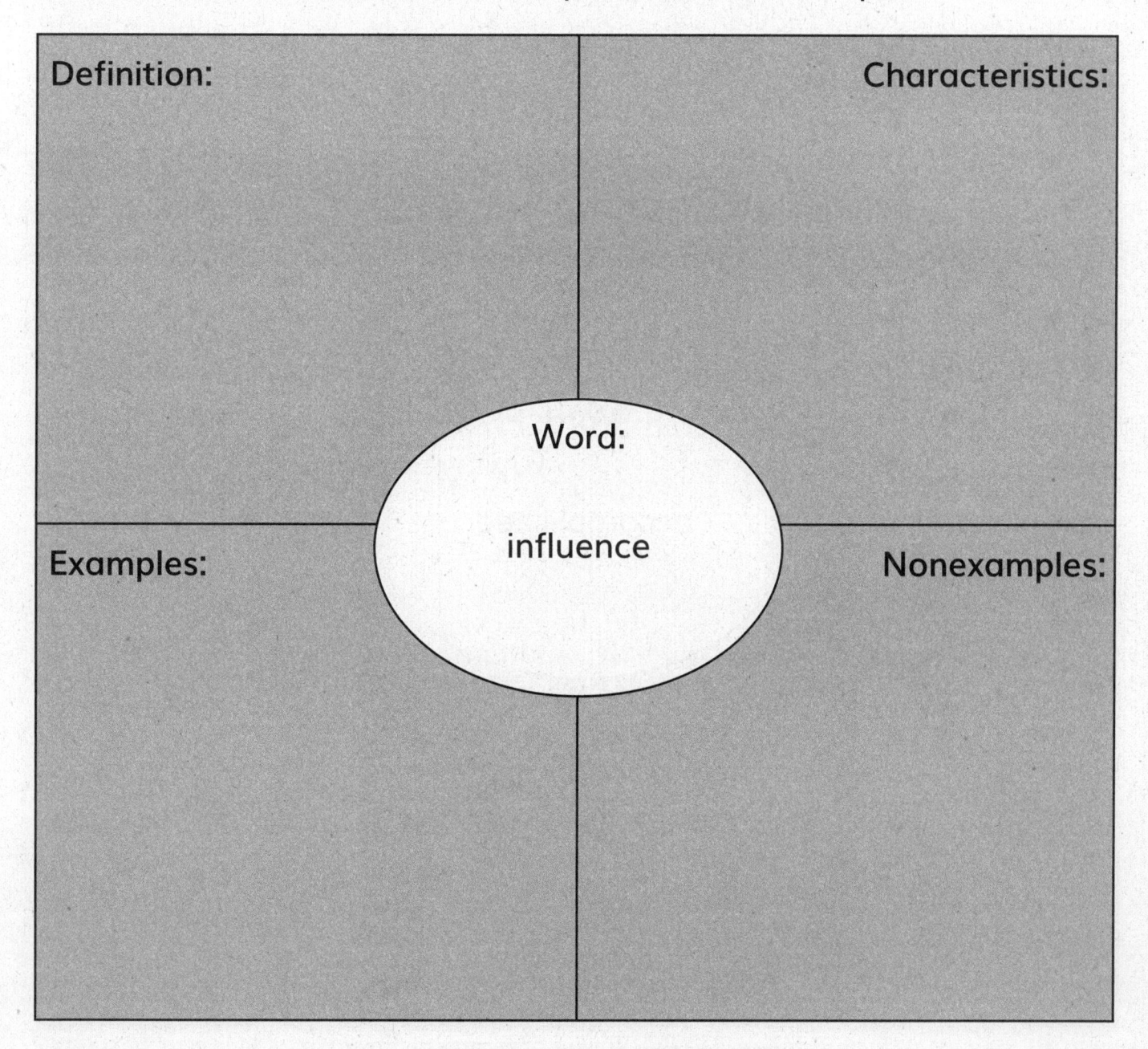

| Definition: | Characteristics: |
|---|---|
| Examples: | Nonexamples: |

Word: influence

# Handout 9A: Frayer Model

**Directions:** Using a dictionary, chart the multiple meanings of the word *accomplished*, and complete the Frayer Model for the word with definitions, characteristics, examples, and nonexamples.

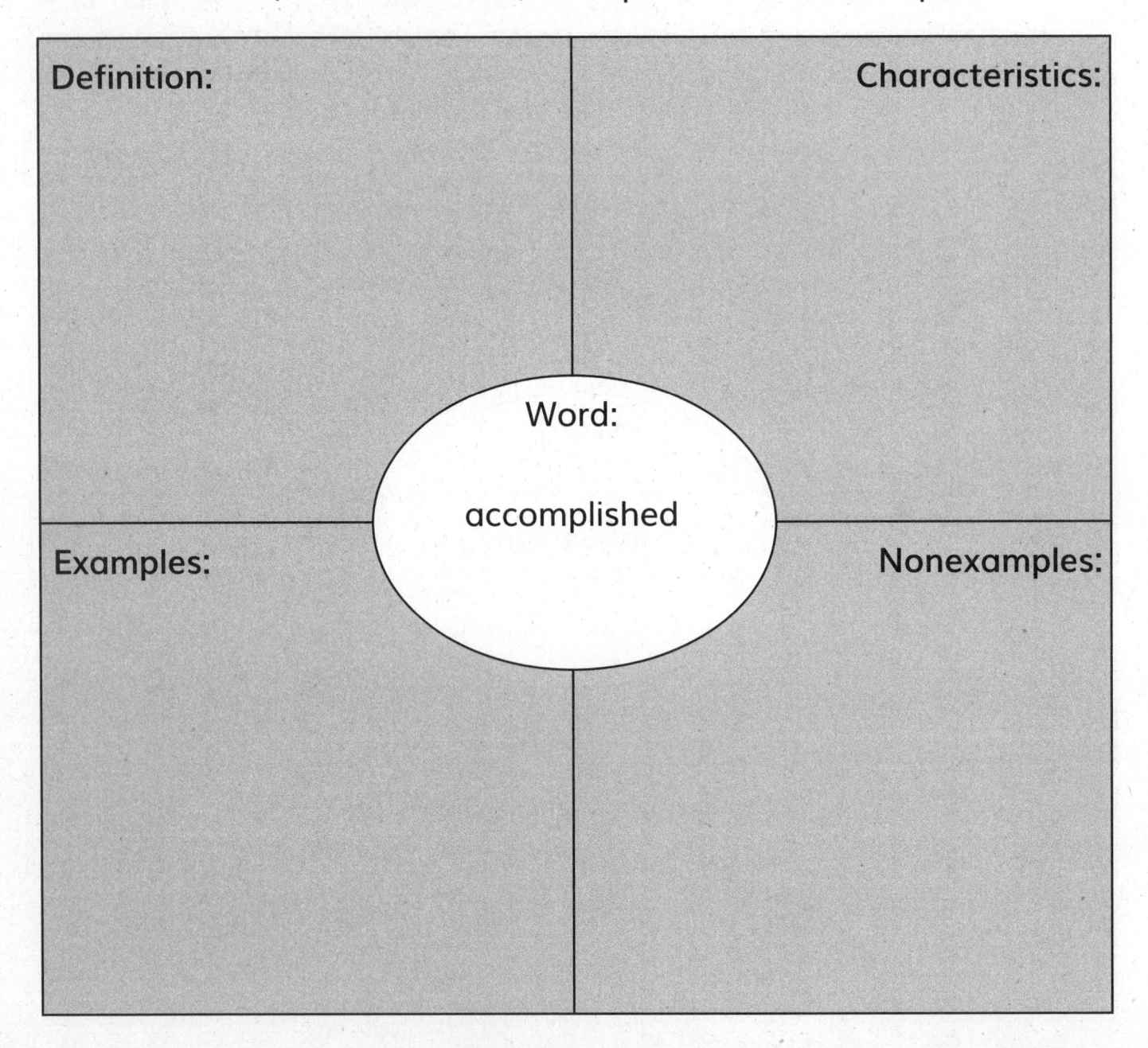

| Definition: | Characteristics: |
|---|---|
| Examples: | Nonexamples: |

Word: accomplished

# Name

# Handout 9A: Frayer Model

**Directions:** Using a dictionary, chart the multiple meanings of the word *believed*, and complete the Frayer Model for the word with definitions, characteristics, examples, and nonexamples.

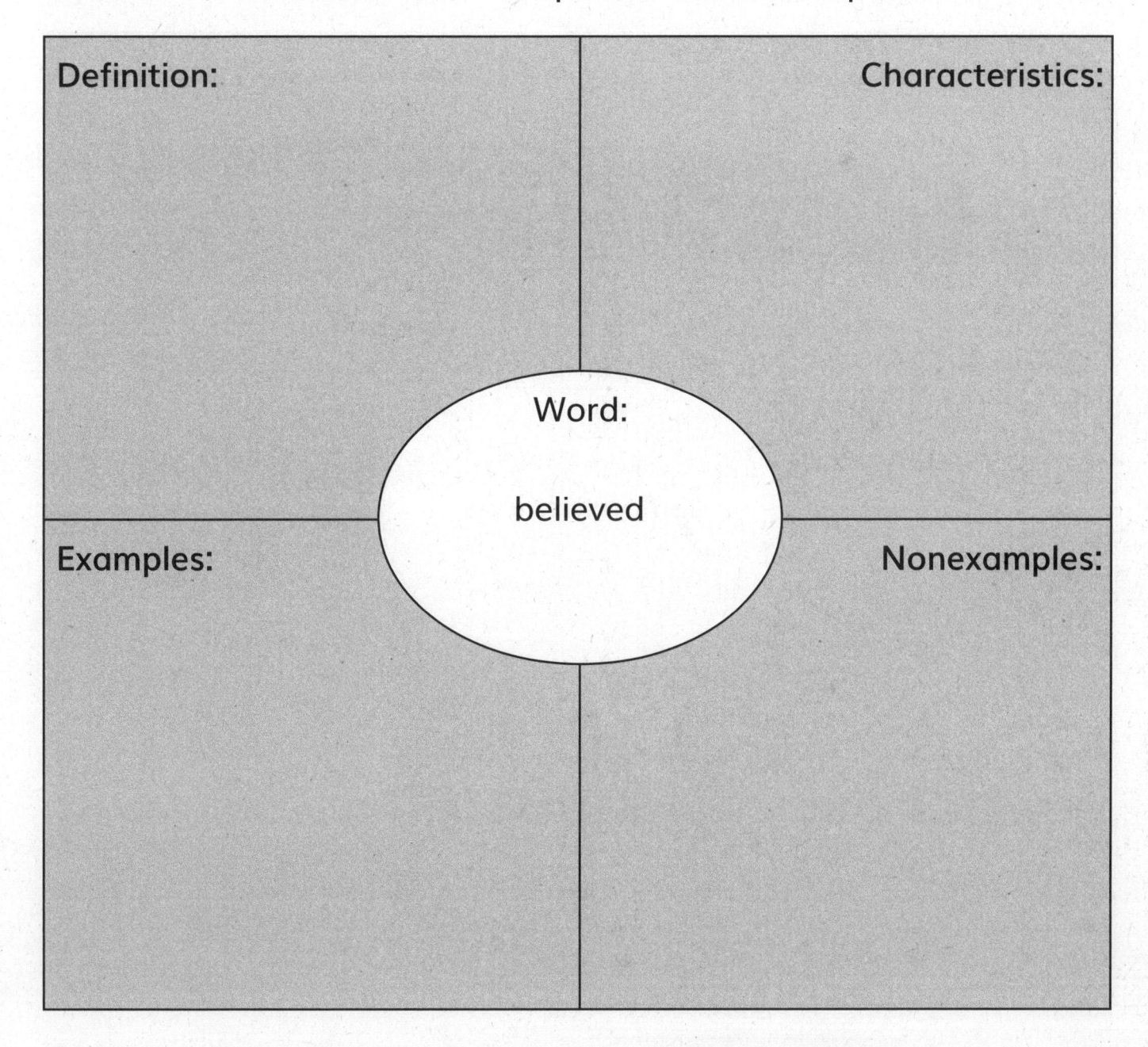

| Definition: | Characteristics: |
|---|---|
| Examples: | Nonexamples: |

Word: believed

# Handout 9A: Frayer Model

**Directions:** Using a dictionary, chart the multiple meanings of the word *demonstrations*, and complete the Frayer Model for the word with definitions, characteristics, examples, and nonexamples.

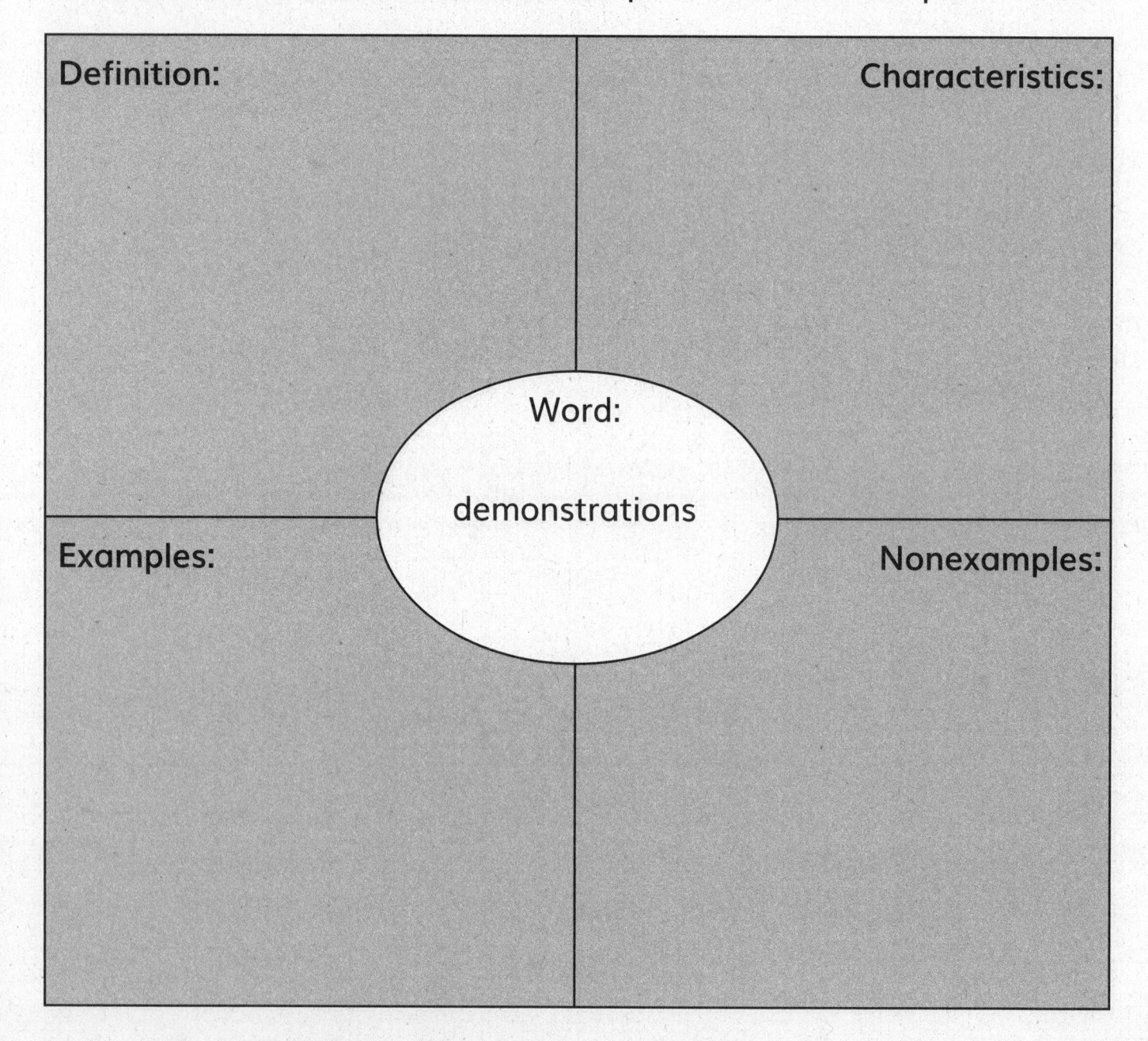

| Definition: | Characteristics: |
|---|---|
| | |

Word: demonstrations

| Examples: | Nonexamples: |
|---|---|
| | |

# Name

# Handout 9A: Frayer Model

**Directions:** Using a dictionary, chart the multiple meanings of the vocabulary word, and complete the Frayer Model for the word with definitions, characteristics, examples, and nonexamples.

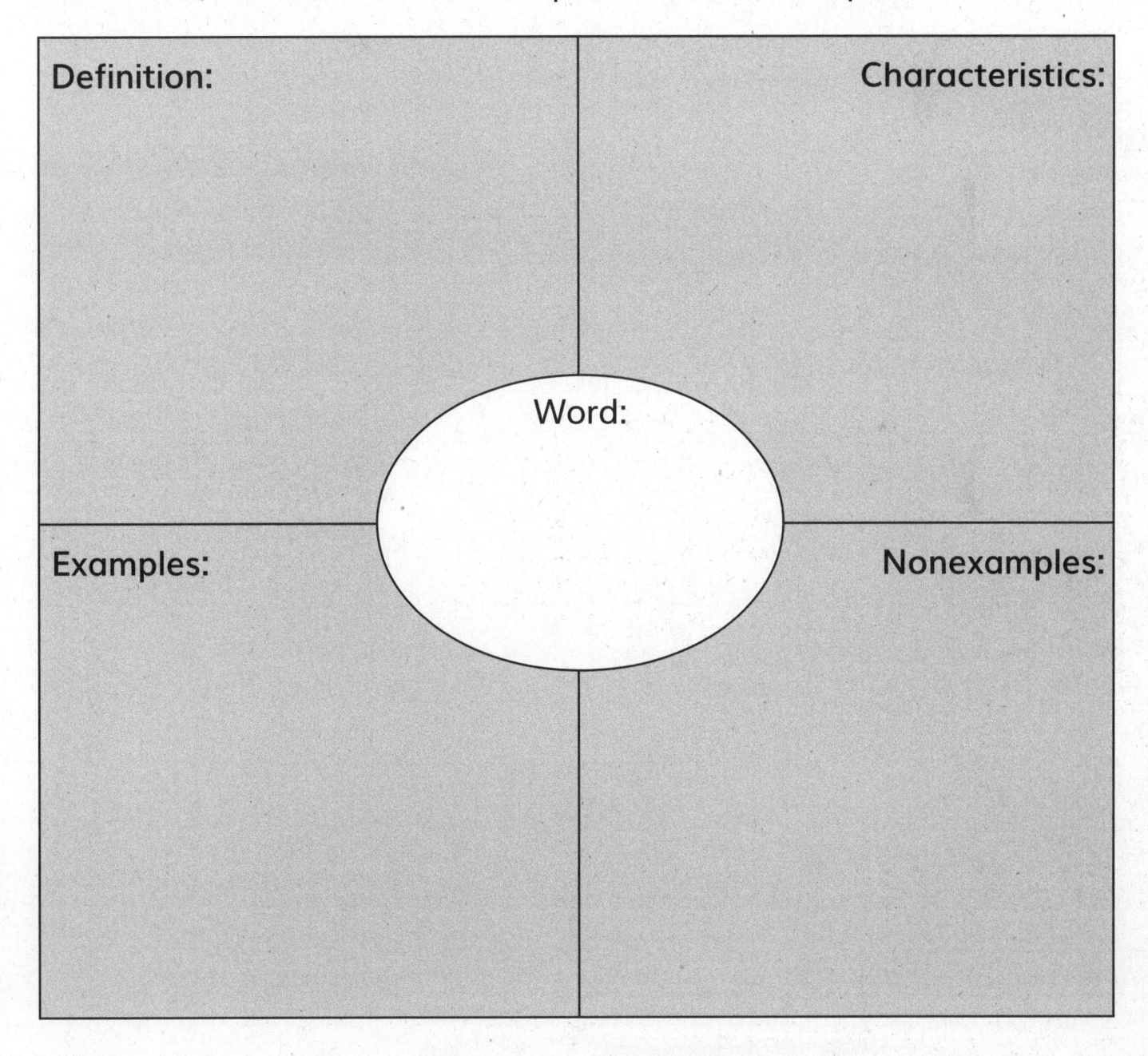

| Definition: | Characteristics: |
|---|---|
| Examples: | Nonexamples: |

Word:

# Name _____

# Handout 10A: Socratic Seminar Participation Guidelines

- Take turns speaking.

- Listen carefully to others by tracking the speaker.

- Listen so you can restate the speaker's ideas.

- Speak at least once.

- Speak to one another, not to the teacher, by turning your eyes and bodies toward one another.

- Ask questions.

- Explain your thinking in light of the discussion.

## Ways to Participate in Socratic Seminar

- Take a risk.

- Ask a question.

- Ask a follow-up question.

- Practice active listening.

- Provide evidence.

- Smile and have fun.

- Stay focused.

# Name

# Handout 10B:
# Socratic Seminar Self-Assessment

**Directions:** Complete this chart by using one of the letters from the key to describe how often you performed the described action. In the last column, explain why you selected the letter you did.

A = I always did that.

S = I sometimes did that.

N = I'll do that next time.

| Expectation | Evaluation (A, S, N) | Evidence: Why did you choose that rating? |
|---|---|---|
| I came to the seminar prepared and used my work as I participated in the seminar. | | |
| I followed our class rules and expectations for the seminar, including any specific role I was assigned. | | |

| | | |
|---|---|---|
| I agreed and disagreed respectfully. | | |
| I asked and answered questions that made our discussion clearer and linked others' ideas together. | | |
| I explained my own ideas using the connections I made from listening to others. | | |
| I spoke in complete sentences. | | |
| I used at least three domain-specific vocabulary words. | | |
| I provided evidence from the texts in this module to support my points. | | |

# Name

# Handout 10C: Conclusion Paragraph Writing Checklist

**Directions:** Use this checklist to review your writing and a peer's writing. Use the revision annotations that follow to make any changes you think will improve the writing. Mark + for "yes" and ∆ for "not yet" to evaluate your work and a peer's work. Ask someone (adult or peer) to evaluate your writing as well.

| Structure | Self +/∆ | Peer +/∆ | Teacher +/∆ |
|---|---|---|---|
| I restated the topic statement. | | | |
| I included key points from the essay. | | | |
| I explained why the topic matters. | | | |
| **Conventions** | | | |
| I used complete sentences. | | | |
| I capitalized titles correctly. | | | |
| **Writing Process** | | | |
| I provided thoughtful feedback in peer revision. | | | |
| I used feedback in peer revision. | | | |
| Total number of +'s | | | |

**Revision Annotations:**

∧     = insert

----   = delete

/     = lower case

=     = upper case

# Name

# Handout 11A: Speaking and Listening Process Checklist

**Directions:** Use the checklist below to monitor how well you used your speaking and listening skills. Then ask a classmate to evaluate how well you used the skills. Your teacher will complete the third column, based on what they observe.

| Speaking and Listening Process Checklist | | | |
|---|---|---|---|
| | Self +/ Δ | Peer +/ Δ | Teacher +/ Δ |
| I took turns speaking and listening. | | | |
| I followed all the rules for working in a small group. | | | |
| I linked my comments to comments from other people. | | | |

| | | | |
|---|---|---|---|
| I agreed and disagreed respectfully. | | | |
| • I used a polite tone of voice throughout the discussion. | | | |
| • I used a sentence stem to help me agree or disagree respectfully. | | | |
| • I used a nonverbal cue to show that I agreed or disagreed with a speaker. | | | |
| I explained my thinking in light of our discussion. | | | |
| I used appropriate facts and details to report on a topic or text. | | | |
| I spoke clearly at an understandable pace. | | | |
| My comments showed that I am curious about what we are learning. | | | |
| My comments showed that I can recount what others say. | | | |

# Name

# Handout 11B: Describe Your Knowledge "To a Tee" Writing Planner

**Directions:** Use this graphic organizer to plan your response to Focusing Question Task 1.

| I | Introduce Topic | |
|---|---|---|
| \multicolumn{3}{c}{Body Paragraph 1} |
| T | Topic Statement | |
| E | Evidence (Fact, Definition, or Detail) | |
| E | Elaboration | |

| Body Paragraph 2 ||  |
|---|---|---|
| T | Topic Statement | |
| E | Evidence (Fact, Definition, or Detail) | |
| E | Elaboration | |
| C | Conclusion | |

# Name

# Handout 11C: Deconstructing Compound Sentences

**Directions:** Choose a compound sentence, and write it here:

Circle the conjunction.

Write the simple sentence that you see before the conjunction in the box labeled "Simple Sentence 1."

Write the simple sentence that you see after the conjunction in the box labeled "Simple Sentence 2."

Record the coordinating conjunction that combines the simple sentences.

Explain how the second part of the compound sentence (Simple Sentence 2) connects to the first part of the compound sentence (Simple Sentence 1). Once the sentence has been deconstructed, you will analyze how the second sentence connects to the first with a partner.

| | |
|---|---|
| **Simple Sentence 1** | |
| **Coordinating Conjunction** | |
| **Simple Sentence 2** | |
| **How does sentence 2 connect to sentence 1?** | |

# Name

# Handout 12A:
# Focusing Question Task 1 Checklist

**Directions:** Use this checklist to revise your writing. Mark + for "yes" and Δ for "not yet." Ask someone (adult or peer) to evaluate your writing as well. Then answer the questions at the bottom of the page.

| Informative/Explanatory Writing Checklist | | | |
|---|---|---|---|
| | Self +/ Δ | Peer +/ Δ | Teacher +/ Δ |
| **Reading Comprehension** | | | |
| • I clearly explained the relationship between events or ideas. | | | |
| **Structure** | | | |
| • I responded to all parts of the prompt. | | | |
| • I focused on my topic. | | | |
| • I introduced the topic in my introductory paragraph. | | | |
| • I organized information about my topic into groups. | | | |
| • My concluding section refers to my topic. | | | |

| | | | |
|---|---|---|---|
| **Development** | | | |
| • I developed my topic with evidence from text(s). | | | |
| • I explained or analyzed my topic in detail. | | | |
| **Style** | | | |
| • I used adjectives to elaborate and to clearly explain my ideas. | | | |
| • I used vocabulary words that are appropriate to the topic. | | | |
| • I used and circled at least two new vocabulary words. | | | |
| • My writing is appropriate for the purpose and audience of the task. | | | |
| **Conventions** | | | |
| • I used correct capitalization and punctuation. | | | |
| **Writing Process** | | | |
| • I used a Writing Planner to organize my ideas. | | | |
| • I provided thoughtful feedback in peer revision. | | | |
| • I used feedback in peer revision. | | | |
| **Total number of +'s:** | | | |

# Name

When you have finished reviewing your work, underline one adjective in your essay. Use the space below to explain how the adjective functions in your sentence.

Adjective:

How does the adjective function in the sentence?

# Name

# Handout 12B:
# Using Compound Sentences

**Directions:** Revise the paragraph below to express the ideas more clearly and to show how the ideas are related.

As you revise, be sure to:

- Combine simple sentences into compound sentences.
- Use at least two different coordinating conjunctions.

Use the following annotation codes as you revise:

/ = lower case

∧ = insert

People believed tradition. The earth was the center of the universe. The sun, moon, and other planets revolved around Earth. Copernicus discovered the earth moves. He could not prove it. Galileo was a curious child. He studied mathematics and physics. Galileo loved stars. He studied the stars. He wrote down his observations. He published a book. People were amazed. People celebrated Galileo. He became famous. The church was worried. Galileo went against the church. He was tried in the pope's court. Galileo was afraid. He was punished. Galileo spent the rest of his life in his house. He never stopped thinking about stars. The church pardoned Galileo three hundred years later.

# Name

# Handout 13A: Fluency Homework

**Directions:**

1. Day 1: Read the text carefully, and annotate to help you read fluently.

2. Each day:
    a. Practice reading the text aloud three to five times.
    b. Evaluate your progress by placing a √+, √, or √- in the appropriate, unshaded box.
    c. Ask someone (adult or peer) to listen and to evaluate your reading.

3. Last day: Fill out the Self-reflection section at the end.

## Moonshot: The Flight of Apollo 11
## by Brian Floca

Then Armstrong and Aldrin climb down from the Eagle in heavy gloves, in large, round helmets, in suits not made for Earth—in suits made for the Moon, here below, all around them, cold and quiet, no air, but life—there is life on the strange and silent, magnificent Moon.

Armstrong and Aldrin walk its rough, wide places. They step, they hop. As light as boys, they lope, they leap!

In the dust and stone beneath their feet, no seed has ever grown, no root has ever reached. Still secrets wait there, the story of the Moon:

Where did it come from? How old is it? What is it made of? (Not green cheese.)

---

Floca, Brian. *Moonshot: The Flight of Apollo 11*. Atheneum Books for Young Readers, 2009, pp. [31–32].

# Name

| Student Performance Checklist | Day 1 You | Day 1 Listener* | Day 2 You | Day 2 Listener* | Day 3 You | Day 3 Listener* | Day 4 You | Day 4 Listener* |
|---|---|---|---|---|---|---|---|---|
| Accurately read the passage three to five times. | | | | | | | | |
| Read with appropriate phrasing and pausing. | ▓ | ▓ | | | | | | |
| Read with appropriate expression. | ▓ | ▓ | ▓ | ▓ | | | | |
| Read articulately at a good pace and an audible volume. | ▓ | ▓ | ▓ | ▓ | ▓ | ▓ | | |

*Adult or peer

**Self-reflection:** What choices did you make when deciding how to read this passage, and why? What would you like to improve on or try to do differently next time? (Thoughtfully answer these questions on the back of this paper.)

# Name

# Handout 14A:
# Illustration Details in *Moonshot*

**Directions:** With your group, study the illustrations on your assigned pages in *Moonshot*. Notice the details that Brian Floca chose to include when illustrating the events of the Apollo 11 mission. List the details in the Illustration Details column. Then, briefly explain how the illustrations add to your understanding of the event.

| Event and Pages | Number of Pages | Illustration Details | How Details Add to Understanding |
|---|---|---|---|
| Planning [4–5] | 2 | | |
| Preparation [6–11] | 6 | | |
| Liftoff [12–17] | 6 | | |

| Event and Pages | Number of Pages | Illustration Details | How Details Add to Understanding |
|---|---|---|---|
| Rocket stages [18–19] | 2 | | |
| Flight to the moon [19–29] | 11 | | |
| Landing of the *Eagle* [30–33] | 4 | | |
| Moon walk [34–41] | 8 | | |
| Return flight [42–45] | 4 | | |
| Splashdown [46–47] | 2 | | |

# Name

# Handout 16A:
# Identifying Points of View

**Directions:**

1. Circle the group on the following page whose point of view you are analyzing.

2. Reread *Moonshot*.

3. As you read, note the pages you are analyzing, record the event(s) described in the text, and explain how the illustration and/or language helps you understand the group's point of view.

   Examples of language that help you understand the point of view might include:

   - Word choice

   - Repetition

   - Onomatopoeia (sound words)

   - Nonliteral language (similes or metaphors)

**Group: Astronauts    Mission Control    Launch Control    Public**

| Pages | Event | Illustration | Language |
|---|---|---|---|
|  |  |  |  |
|  |  |  |  |
|  |  |  |  |
|  |  |  |  |
|  |  |  |  |
|  |  |  |  |
|  |  |  |  |

# Name

# Handout 16B: Tableau Checklist

**Directions:** Select an event from *Moonshot*, and create a Tableau depicting that event.

As you create the Tableau, think about the following questions:

CONTENT:

\_\_\_\_ Does the Tableau depict the group of people we are representing?

\_\_\_\_ Does the Tableau reflect evidence from the text to depict the event accurately?

\_\_\_\_ Have we posed the people in a position that demonstrates their point of view regarding the event?

\_\_\_\_ Have we used a sound effect that allows viewers to understand the point of view of the people in the Tableau better? (Optional)

## PROCESS:

____ Did we follow agreed-upon rules for discussion while were creating the Tableau?

____ Did we agree and disagree respectfully while we were creating the Tableau?

____ Did we speak to explain our ideas while we were creating the Tableau?

# Name

# Handout 17B: Writing Planner

**Directions:** Use this graphic organizer to plan a response to an opinion prompt.

In your opinion, which part of *Moonshot* best depicts the wonder or danger of traveling to the moon?

| I | Introduce Topic | |
|---|---|---|
| O | Opinion Statement | |
| | Body Paragraph 1 | |
| R | Reason | |
| E | Evidence | |
| E | Elaboration | |
| C | Concluding Statement | |
| | Body Paragraph 2 | |
| R | Reason | |
| E | Evidence | |
| E | Elaboration | |
| C | Concluding Statement | |
| | | |
| O | Reinforce Opinion | |

## Part 2

| | |
|---|---|
| Does the introduction identify the text? | |
| Does the introduction identify the author? | |
| Does the introduction state the topic? | |
| Does the introduction provide an opinion and give two supporting reasons? | |

# Handout 18A:
# "Apollo 11: The *Eagle* Has Landed"

**Directions:** Read the article below, and then answer the questions for New-Read Assessment 2.

On July 20, 1969, for the first time in history, human beings stepped onto the Moon. They were American astronauts Neil Armstrong and Edwin "Buzz" Aldrin. "That's one small step for man ... one giant leap for mankind," Armstrong said as he stepped off the ladder. His boots made marks in the dusty grit of the Moon.

The astronauts had brought a television camera with them. So 242,000 miles away, the world heard Armstrong speak those unforgettable words. People watched in amazement as Armstrong took the first steps on the Moon. Moments later, Buzz Aldrin followed Armstrong out of the lunar module. Meanwhile, astronaut Michael Collins continued orbiting the Moon 69 miles above them. He was in the command ship, *Columbia*, which would take the three astronauts home. But for now Aldrin and Armstrong only had eyes for the surface of the Moon. They had done it! They were the first men on the Moon.

Apollo 11 had blasted off from Cape Canaveral, Florida, four days earlier. As the rocket sped them into space, each astronaut's body weight increased to about 1,000 pounds. When the ship finally escaped Earth's gravity, the men became weightless, floating around if they weren't strapped in. It was strange to live in zero gravity—things floated away if they weren't attached to something. The astronauts had to eat and drink through tubes and straws. They couldn't shower. And just imagine going to the bathroom! The men could brush their teeth, but they couldn't spit out the toothpaste. Their faces swelled because blood moved through their bodies in a different way. The astronauts said the ship stank, but no one cared. Only the Moon mattered.

The crew of Apollo 11 had a smooth flight into space. The astronauts had spent hundreds of hours training for this mission. They learned how to operate the equipment and what to do if something went wrong. And Neil Armstrong knew how much could go wrong. On an earlier space mission, his ship had spun wildly. He could have passed out, but he managed to fix the problem.

Four days after leaving Earth, astronauts Armstrong and Aldrin climbed into the small, bug-like lunar module called the *Eagle*. They were ready to go down to the surface of the Moon. But an alarm began to sound. The ship's computer was overloaded with information, setting off the alarm. Then, from mission control back on Earth, the astronauts heard the words they were waiting for: "We're go, Eagle. Hang tight." They launched the Eagle. But a new problem came up: the Eagle passed the landing site. Aldrin told Armstrong the Eagle was nearly out of fuel. Taking the controls, Armstrong coaxed the ship towards a clear area, trying to land before the engine drank the last bit of fuel. With only 16 seconds of fuel left, Armstrong called the control center in Houston. "The Eagle has landed!"

# Name

Armstrong and Aldrin took pictures and collected Moon rocks and dust. They placed scientific equipment on the Moon, and did some experiments. Because there was so little gravity, walking felt more like floating. The astronauts described the Moon as black and gray— beautiful in a desert-like way. When their work was finished, Armstrong and Aldrin fired the special engine that lifted the Eagle off of the Moon. It was time to head back to the blue, brown, and green planet called home.

A few years later Apollo 17 was the last manned mission to the Moon. Astronauts Gene Cernan and Harrison Schmitt landed on the Moon on December 19, 1972. We haven't been back—but wouldn't it be wonderful if we could?

# Name

# Handout 19A:
# Model Opinion Paragraph

**Directions:** Organize the sentences into a model opinion paragraph using the mnemonic "I-OREE-CO."

| I | Introduce Topic | |
|---|---|---|
| O | Opinion Statement | |
| R | Reason | |
| E | Evidence | |
| E | Elaboration | |
| C | Concluding Statement | |

*Moonshot*, by Brian Floca, and *One Giant Leap*, by Robert Burleigh, are both about the Apollo 11 mission.

The reason I think this is that *One Giant Leap* shows that the mission helped the whole world.

In my opinion, *One Giant Leap* does a better job of showing how important the mission was.

The book also reports that the president told Armstrong, "For a priceless moment, all the people on this earth are truly one."

*One Giant Leap* demonstrates how important the Apollo 11 mission was to everyone on Earth.

For example, the book reports that when Armstrong put his foot on the moon, he said, "That's one small step for man—one giant leap for mankind."

# Name

# Handout 19B: Fluency Homework

**Directions:**

1. Day 1: Read the text carefully, and annotate to help you read fluently.

2. Each day:

    a. Practice reading the text aloud three to five times.
    b. Evaluate your progress by placing a √+, √, or √- in the appropriate, unshaded box.
    c. Ask someone (adult or peer) to listen and to evaluate your reading.

3. Last day: Fill out the Self-reflection section at the end.

# One Giant Leap
## by Robert Burleigh

"EAGLE: 90 SECONDS OF DESCENT FUEL LEFT."

Armstrong hears the warning. *Now.* All he has ever learned is focused on this. Nothing matters but this exact moment. Aldrin's nonstop voice calls out altitude numbers: "Forty feet, thirty-five, thirty…" Down they move, down and down. Fast enough to conserve precious fuel. Slow enough to land somewhere safely. He hopes.

The *Eagle* dips. Hovers. Zigs. Zags. Dances over its own dark shadow. The seconds tick toward eternity. Time stops. Clouds of moondust swirl like blackening fog. An almost terrifying blindness. And then—with only the very slightest bump—the small craft touches down. *Whew!*

---

Burleigh, Robert. *One Giant Leap*. Illustrated by Mike Wimmer. Philomel Books, 2009, p. [12].

# Name _____

| Student Performance Checklist | Day 1 You | Day 1 Listener* | Day 2 You | Day 2 Listener* | Day 3 You | Day 3 Listener* | Day 4 You | Day 4 Listener* |
|---|---|---|---|---|---|---|---|---|
| Accurately read the passage three to five times. |  |  |  |  |  |  |  |  |
| Read with appropriate phrasing and pausing. | ▓ | ▓ |  |  |  |  |  |  |
| Read with appropriate expression. | ▓ | ▓ | ▓ | ▓ |  |  |  |  |
| Read articulately at a good pace and an audible volume. | ▓ | ▓ | ▓ | ▓ | ▓ | ▓ |  |  |

*Adult or peer

**Self-reflection:** What choices did you make when deciding how to read this passage, and why? What would you like to improve on or try to do differently next time? (Thoughtfully answer these questions on the back of this paper.)

# Name

# Handout 19C: Frayer Model

**Directions:** Using a dictionary, chart the multiple meanings of the vocabulary word *fragile*, and complete a Frayer Model. Write the definition of the word, along with characteristics, examples, and nonexamples.

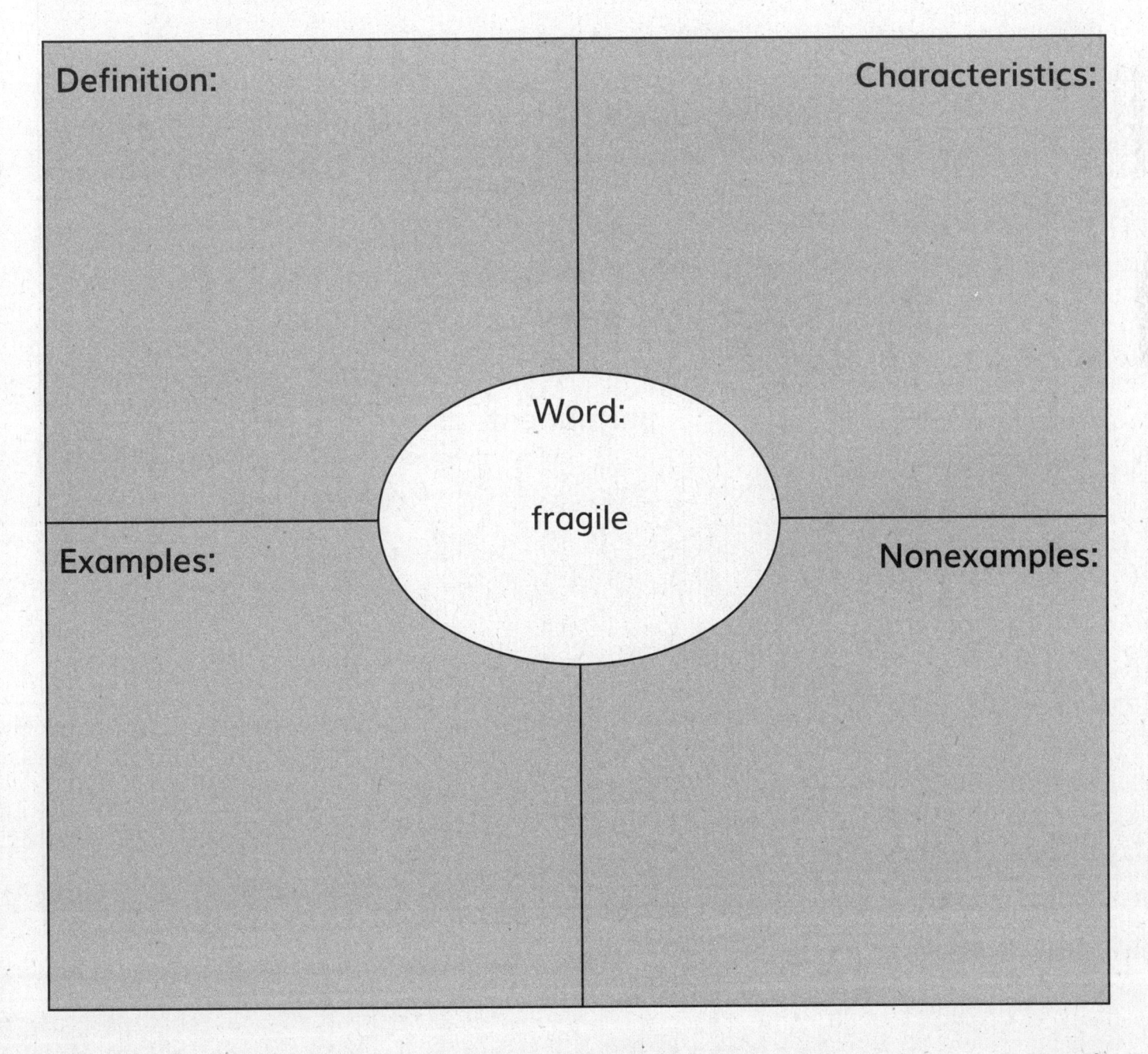

| Definition: | Characteristics: |
|---|---|
| Examples: | Nonexamples: |

Word: fragile

# Handout 19C: Frayer Model

**Directions:** Using a dictionary, chart the multiple meanings of the vocabulary word, *permanent*, and complete a Frayer Model. Write the definition of the word, along with characteristics, examples, and nonexamples.

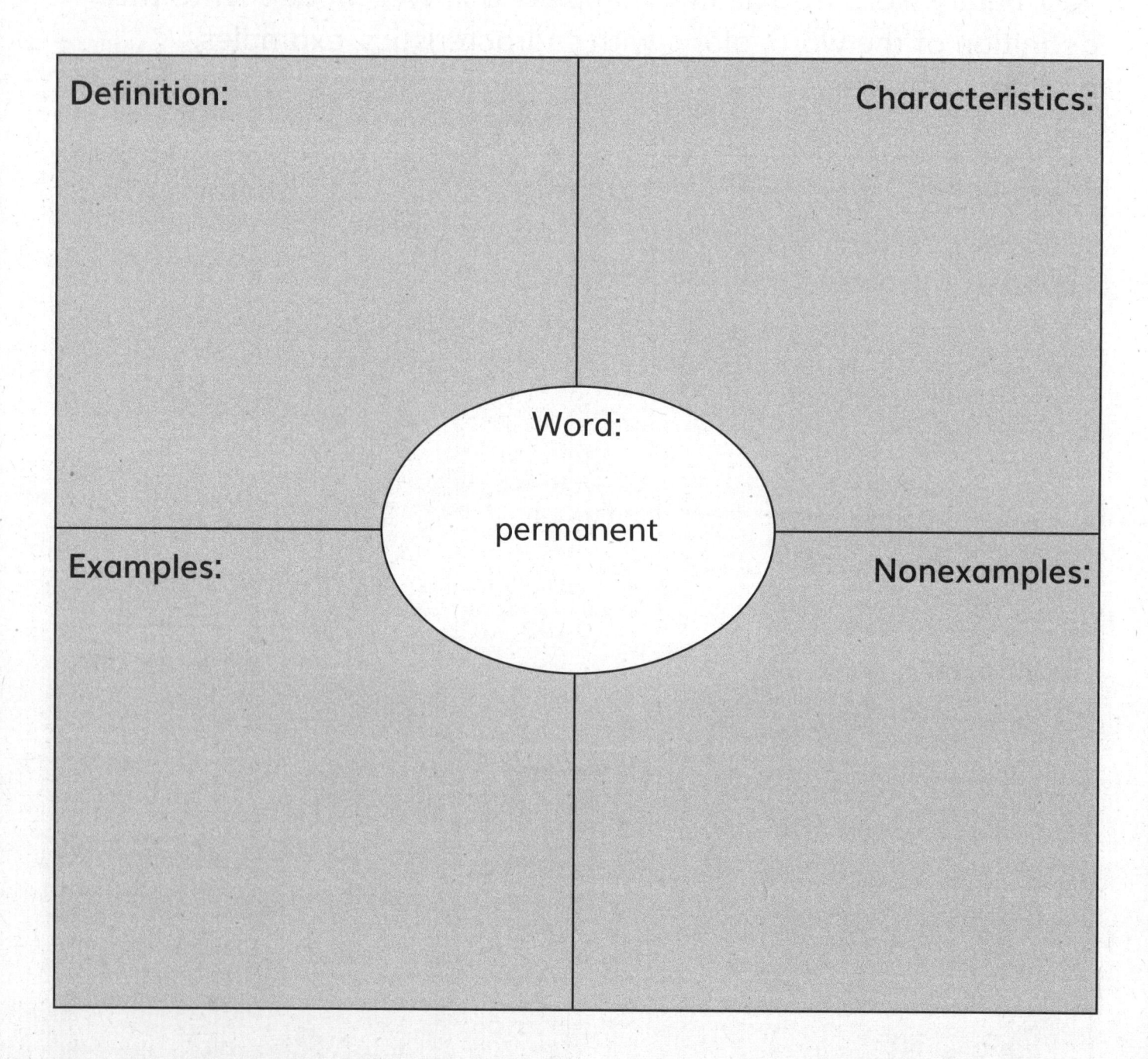

| Definition: | Characteristics: |
|---|---|
| Examples: | Nonexamples: |

Word: permanent

# Name

# Handout 21A: Nonliteral Language in *One Giant Leap*

**Directions:** With your group, choose at least one example of nonliteral language from *One Giant Leap* that helps you understand the Apollo 11 mission better. Record the example you found, along with the page number. In the second column, explain what the nonliteral language means; in the third column, explain how the nonliteral language deepens your understanding of the events of the Apollo 11 mission.

| Example of Nonliteral Language [Page] | What It Means | Analysis: How It Adds Meaning to the Text |
|---|---|---|
| | | |
| | | |
| | | |
| | | |
| | | |
| | | |
| | | |
| | | |

# Name

# Handout 23A: "We Choose the Moon,"

from a speech by President John F. Kennedy

**Directions:** Read the excerpt from John F. Kennedy's speech, and then work with the members of your group to give a fluent performance of the excerpt.

Student 1:   We choose to go to the moon.

Student 2:   We choose to go to the moon in this decade and do the other things,

Student 3:   not because they are easy,

Student 4:   but because they are hard,

Student 5:   because that goal will serve to organize

Student 1:   and measure the best of our energies and skills,

Student 2:   because that challenge is one that we are willing to accept,

Student 3:   one we are unwilling to postpone,

Student 4:   and one which we intend to win,

Student 5:   and the others, too.

All:   We choose to go to the moon.

---

Adapted from

"Address at Rice University on the Nation's Space Effort." *Jfklibrary.org*, www.jfklibrary.org/learn/about-jfk/historic-speeches/address-at-rice-university-on-the-nations-space-effort. Accessed 22 Sept. 2022.

# Name

# Handout 24A: Socratic Seminar Self-Assessment

**Directions:** Complete this chart by using one of the letters from the key to describe how often you performed the described action. In the last column, explain why you selected the letter you did.

A = I always did that.   S = I sometimes did that.   N = I'll do that next time.

| Expectation | Evaluation (A, S, N) | Evidence: Why did you choose that rating? |
|---|---|---|
| I came to the seminar prepared and used my work as I participated in the seminar. | | |
| I followed our class rules and expectations for the seminar, including any specific role I was assigned. | | |
| I agreed and disagreed respectfully. | | |
| I asked and answered questions that made our discussion clearer and linked others' ideas together. | | |

| | | |
|---|---|---|
| I explained my own ideas using the connections I made from listening to others. | | |
| I spoke in complete sentences. | | |
| I used at least three domain-specific vocabulary words. | | |
| I provided evidence from the texts in this module to support my points. | | |
| I can express President Kennedy's point of view in "We Choose the Moon." | | |
| I can express my point and how it is different or similar to President Kennedy's. | | |

# Name

# Handout 24B:
# Taking Apart "We Choose the Moon"

**Directions:**

1. Cut the clauses into separate strips.

2. Cut apart the coordinating and subordinating conjunctions.

3. Arrange the clauses in an order that makes sense.

4. Use the conjunctions to create compound and complex sentences.

5. Glue or tape your sentences onto a piece of paper.

6. Add the correct punctuation and capitalization.

| |
|---|
| they are hard |
| we choose to go to the moon |
| we choose to go to the moon in this decade and do the other things |
| that challenge is one that we are willing to accept |
| they are easy |
| that goal will serve to organize and measure the best of our energies and skills |

| | | | |
|---|---|---|---|
| and | but | or | for |
| nor | yet | so | because |
| therefore | although | if | then |

# Name

# Handout 25A: Comparing and Contrasting Texts

**Directions:** As you prepare for the Focusing Question Task 2 Assessment, review *Moonshot* and *One Giant Leap* to compare how the authors present the events of the Apollo 11 mission. Consider the events the authors describe and how the authors use illustrations and language to present the advantages and disadvantages of traveling to the moon. Choose at least one example for each criterion. Use extra paper if you need more space.

On the back of this sheet, compare and contrast how *Moonshot* and *One Giant Leap* describe one important event or detail. (RI.3.9)

## This planner will be assessed as part of Focusing Question Task 2.

| *Moonshot*, Brian Floca | | |
|---|---|---|
| | Advantages | Disadvantages |
| Events that show the advantages and disadvantages of space travel | | far away, on air and no life, and cold and quiet |
| Illustrations that show the advantages and disadvantages of space travel | | no night or day |
| Language that shows the advantages and disadvantages of space travel | | High above the sky |
| *One Giant Leap*, Robert Burleigh | | |
| Events that show the advantages and disadvantages of space travel | | but this is no escape from this no backing up no doig |
| Illustrations that show the advantages and disadvantages of space travel | | |
| Language that shows the advantages and disadvantages of space travel | | |

# Name

# Handout 25B: Writing Planner

**Directions:** Use this graphic organizer to plan a response to Focusing Question Task 2.

You are entering an opinion essay content. The essays will be judged by scientists and artists. The question that you have to answer in your essay is: Would you like to have been an astronaut on the Apollo 11 mission?

| I | Introduce Topic | |
|---|---|---|
| O | Opinion Statement | I don't want to go to the moon. |
| | **Body Paragraph 1 –** | Moonshot |
| R | Reason | Space is dangerous, hard, fall. |
| E | Evidence | No air, no life, no food, no toliets. |
| E | Elaboration | I will crash and broke my bones on the moon |
| C | Concluding Statement | is one that moon is bad. |

|   |   | Body Paragraph 2 One giant leap |
|---|---|---|
| R | Reason | I would not go |
| E | Evidence | because is death |
| E | Elaboration | If I will Jump hard I will flip |
| C | Concluding Statement | not to go on the moon |
|   |   |   |
| O | Reinforce Opinion |   |

## Part 2

| Does the introduction identify the text? |   |
|---|---|
| Does the introduction identify the author? |   |
| Does the introduction state the topic? |   |
| Does the introduction provide an opinion and give two supporting reasons? |   |

# Name

# Handout 26A:
# Focusing Question Task 2 Checklist

**Directions:** Use this checklist to revise your writing. Mark + for "yes" and Δ for "not yet." Ask someone (adult or peer) to evaluate your writing as well. Then answer the questions at the bottom of the page.

| Grade 3 Opinion Writing Checklist | | | |
|---|---|---|---|
| | Self +/ Δ | Peer +/ Δ | Teacher +/ Δ |
| **Structure** | | | |
| • I responded to all parts of the prompt. | | | |
| • I focused on my opinion. | | | |
| • I introduced the topic or text in my introductory paragraph. | | | |
| • I stated an opinion. | | | |
| • I organized or listed my reasons in a way that makes sense. | | | |
| **Development** | | | |
| • I supported my opinion with reasons, using evidence from Handout 25A. | | | |

| | | | |
|---|---|---|---|
| **Style** | | | |
| • I used simple and compound sentences. | | | |
| • I used vocabulary words that are appropriate to the topic. | | | |
| • I used and circled at least three new vocabulary words. | | | |
| • My writing is appropriate for the purpose and audience of the task. | | | |
| **Conventions** | | | |
| • I used adjectives to elaborate and to clearly explain my ideas. | | | |
| • I used adverbs to elaborate and to clearly explain my ideas. | | | |
| • I used coordinating conjunctions that are appropriate to create compound sentences. | | | |
| **Writing Process** | | | |
| • I used a Writing Planner to organize my ideas. | | | |
| • I provided thoughtful feedback in peer revision. | | | |
| • I used feedback in peer revision. | | | |
| Total number of +'s: | | | |

# Name

When you have finished reviewing your work, underline one adverb in your essay. In the space below, explain how the adverb functions in the sentence.

Adverb:

How does the adverb function in the sentence?

# Name

# Handout 27A: Story Map

**Directions:** Use this chart to organize and record notes about key details in the story.

| Character(s): | Setting: |
|---|---|
| | |

**Conflict(s):**
*The main problem in this part of the story is ...*

**Event Timeline:** *(Attempts to Solve the Problem)*

*First ...*

*Next ...*

*Then ...*

*After that ...*

**Resolution:**

**Central Message:**

**Supporting Key Details:**

- 

-

# Name

# Handout 27B: Fluency Homework

**Directions:**

1. Day 1: Read the text carefully, and annotate to help you read fluently.

2. Each day:

    a. Practice reading the text aloud three to five times.
    b. Evaluate your progress by placing a √+, √, or √- in the appropriate, unshaded box.
    c. Ask someone (adult or peer) to listen and to evaluate your reading.

3. Last day: Fill out the Self-reflection section at the end.

# Zathura

## by Chris Van Allsburg

"See," said Danny, "outer space." He led Walter back to the living room and showed him the Zathura game board and the card. Walter sat with his head in his hands, gazing at the path of colored squares that wound around the board and ended back at Earth.

"Looks like," said Danny, "we keep on playing or we're up here forever."

"Great," said Walter. "Up here, with you, forever." He took a deep breath, put a token on Earth, then rolled the dice and moved along the path. The board started buzzing, and—click—a card popped out. He studied it silently, then tossed the card on the board.

Danny leaned forward and read: "'The polarity on your gravity belt is reversed.'" I wonder what that means?" He looked up, but Walter was gone.

---

Van Allsburg, Chris. *Zathura*. Houghton Mifflin Harcourt, 2002, p. [12].

# Name

| Student Performance Checklist | Day 1 You | Day 1 Listener* | Day 2 You | Day 2 Listener* | Day 3 You | Day 3 Listener* | Day 4 You | Day 4 Listener* |
|---|---|---|---|---|---|---|---|---|
| Accurately read the passage three to five times. | | | | | | | | |
| Read with appropriate phrasing and pausing. | | | | | | | | |
| Read with appropriate expression. | | | | | | | | |
| Read articulately at a good pace and an audible volume. | | | | | | | | |

*Adult or peer

**Self-reflection:** What choices did you make when deciding how to read this passage, and why? What would you like to improve on or try to do differently next time? (Thoughtfully answer these questions on the back of this paper.)

# Name

# Handout 27C: Morpheme Matrix

**Directions:** Write a vocabulary term in the space below. Then record the root word in the middle column, along with the definition of the root word. Continue to break apart the term by further separating the suffix and prefix and recording their definitions. In the second row, brainstorm additional words with the same prefix, root, and suffix to see how the morphemes grow.

Vocabulary term: _____

| Prefix | Root | Suffix |
|---|---|---|
|  |  |  |
| List words with same prefix: | List words with same root: | List words with same suffix: |

# Name

# Handout 30A: "Pegasus and Perseus" and "Pegasus and Bellerophon"

**Directions:** Read the text below, and use the Word Box to help you with the words that are **underlined.** Circle unknown words that are not in the Word Box and that you cannot figure out from context.

## Pegasus and Perseus

Long ago in ancient Greece, a young hero named Perseus was sent to destroy a dangerous monster. The monster, Medusa, was frighteningly ugly, with snakes growing out of her head. Merely looking at her caused death, and she had already killed many brave men. Perseus knew it would be difficult to kill Medusa. He asked Athena, the goddess of wisdom, for advice. Athena told Perseus not to look at Medusa's face. Instead, Athena told Perseus to look at Medusa's reflection in his shield. Perseus thanked Athena and set off to find Medusa.

When Perseus finally found Medusa, she was surrounded by statues, the men she had turned to stone when they dared to look at her. Perseus crept up, and looking only at her reflection, chopped off her head. He was amazed when Pegasus, a beautiful winged horse, as white as the purest snow, **emerged** from the neck of the **hideous** monster. Perseus immediately jumped on the horse's back and both Perseus and Pegasus escaped from Medusa's garden of death.

Adapted from

"Greek Myths." *American Museum of Natural History*, www.amnh.org/exhibitions/mythic-creatures/air/greek-myths. Accessed 21 Sept. 2022.

## Pegasus and Bellerophon

   Bellerophon was a brave and proud Greek hero. He was sent to kill the terrifying Chemira. The Chemira was a fire-breathing monster with the head of a lion, the tail of a snake, and the body of a goat. A wise man told Bellerophon that to succeed, he would need to capture Pegasus, the flying horse. The wise man told Bellerophon to ask for help from the goddess Athena. Athena gave Bellerophon a golden bridle and the wise man told him where to find Pegasus. Bellerophon tamed Pegasus and the two flew off to find the Chemira. They killed the terrible monster and went on to share many other adventures.

   As Bellerophon's success grew, so did his pride. He decided to fly on the back of Pegasus to Mount Olympus, home of the gods. Zeus, king of the gods, grew angry when he saw the mortal coming near. He sent a fly down to bite Pegasus. Pegasus **reared** back and Bellerophon tumbled back to Earth, like a pebble tossed from a mountain top. Pegasus continued on to Mount Olympus. On Olympus, Pegasus served Zeus by carrying his lightning bolt. When Pegasus finally died, Zeus turned him into a beautiful **constellation**. You can still see Pegasus, shining in the night sky, if you look up and search for the beautiful winged horse.

Adapted from

"Greek Myths." *American Museum of Natural History*, www.amnh.org/exhibitions/mythic-creatures/air/greek-myths. Accessed 21 Sept. 2022.

# Name

---

Word Box

*emerged*—came out of

*hideous*—very ugly

*constellation*—arrangement of stars that seems to make a picture and that is named for that picture

*reared*—rose up on back legs

# Name _____

# Handout 30B: Recounting a Myth

**Directions:** Work with a partner to complete the story map below and circle the elements that help you identify the story as a map.

Then exchange papers with a partner, and take turns recounting the myth orally. Place a checkmark next to each piece of information on your partner's Story Map that they include while recounting the myth.

| Character(s): | Setting: |
|---|---|
|  |  |

**Conflict(s):**
*The main problem in this part of the story is ...*

**Event Timeline:** *(Attempts to Solve the Problem)*

*First ...*

*Next ...*

*Then ...*

*After that ...*

**Resolution:**

# Name

# Handout 30C: Speaking and Listening Process Checklist

**Directions:** Use the checklist below to monitor how well you used your speaking and listening skills. Then ask a classmate to evaluate how well you used the skills. Your teacher will complete the third column, based on what they observe.

| Grade 3 Speaking and Listening Process Checklist | | | |
|---|---|---|---|
| | Self +/ Δ | Peer +/ Δ | Teacher +/ Δ |
| I took turns speaking and listening. | | | |
| I followed all the rules for working in a small group. | | | |
| I linked my comments to comments from other people. | | | |
| I agreed and disagreed respectfully. | | | |
| • I used a polite tone of voice throughout the discussion. | | | |
| • I used a sentence stem to help me agree or disagree respectfully. | | | |
| • I used a nonverbal cue to show that I agreed or disagreed with a speaker. | | | |

| | | | |
|---|---|---|---|
| I explained my thinking in light of our discussion. | | | |
| I used appropriate facts and details to report on a topic or text. | | | |
| I spoke clearly at an understandable pace. | | | |
| My comments showed that I am curious about what we are learning. | | | |
| My comments showed that I can recount what others say. | | | |

# Name

# Handout 31A:
# Organizer for Research Notes

**Directions:** Record the question your group is researching about the moon. Each member of the group must find a piece of evidence that answers the questions. Then, record the source title and evidence in the chart below. At the bottom, write a three-to-four-sentence summary explaining what you learned about the moon from your research.

| Our Guiding Question About the Moon: | | |
|---|---|---|
| Source: | Source: | Source: |
| Evidence: | Evidence: | Evidence: |
| Initials: | Initials: | Initials: |

**What we learned from our research :**

# Name

# Handout 32A: Socratic Seminar Self-Assessment

**Directions:** Complete this chart by using one of the letters from the key to describe how often you performed the described action. In the last column, explain why you selected the letter you did.

A = I always did that.   S = I sometimes did that.   N = I'll do that next time.

| Expectation | Evaluation (A, S, N) | Evidence: Why did you choose that rating? |
|---|---|---|
| I came to the seminar prepared and used my work as I participated in the seminar. | | |
| I followed our class rules and expectations for the seminar, including any specific role I was assigned. | | |
| I agreed and disagreed respectfully. | | |

| | | |
|---|---|---|
| I asked and answered questions that made our discussion clearer and linked others' ideas together. | | |
| I explained my own ideas using the connections I made from listening to others. | | |
| I spoke in complete sentences. | | |
| I used at least three domain-specific vocabulary words. | | |
| I provided evidence from the texts in this module to support my points. | | |

# Name

# Handout 32B: Vocabulary Study Guide

**Directions:** Draw a picture or write a sentence for the first fifteen words (up through *influence*), using the picture or sentence to help you remember what each word means. You will complete the last fifteen words in Lesson 35. Then glue this paper into your Vocabulary Journal.

| Word | Meaning | Illustration or Sentence |
|---|---|---|
| grit | Small coarse bits of sand or stone. | |
| descent | The act of climbing downward. | |
| gouged | Cut or carved with. | |
| fragile | Easily broken; delicate. | |
| intend | To have a plan in your mind to do something. | |
| malfunctioning | Failing to operate or function. | |

| | | |
|---|---|---|
| myth | A story, often about gods or supernatural characters, passed down through generations to explain something about the world. | |
| constellation | An arrangement of stars that seems to make a picture and that is named for that picture. | |
| condemned | Ordered punishment to be given to; sentenced or convicted. | |
| conserve | To protect something from being destroyed or harmed. | |
| assembly | The coming together of people for a particular purpose. | |
| thrived | Grown with great health or success. | |
| clipped | Of speech, rapidly articulated so as to omit certain sounds. | |

# Name

| permanent | Lasting, or intended to last forever. | |
| influence | The ability to cause a person or thing to change without physically acting. | |
| astronomer | A scientist who studies space. | |
| pardoned | Released someone from the legal consequences of a crime. | |
| accomplished | 1. Done; 2. Skillful; 3. Very able. | |
| hideous | Looking very ugly or frightening; disgusting. | |
| reduced | Made smaller in amount or size. | |
| lunar | Having to do with or related to the moon. | |

| | | |
|---|---|---|
| released | Set something or someone free. | |
| traditions | Practices or beliefs passed down through generations of a culture or group of people. | |
| revolve | To travel in a circle around a specific point. | |
| mission | A special job given to a person or group of people. | |
| advantages | Helpful things | |
| satellites | Objects in the sky that move around another larger object. | |

# Name

| punished | Treated someone in a harsh way because of something they did wrong. | |
|---|---|---|
| doubt | To not be sure of something. | |
| ascent | The act of climbing up to a summit; rise. | |

# Name

# Handout 33A: Writing Planner

**Directions:** Use this graphic organizer to plan a response to Focusing Question Task 3.

| | | |
|---|---|---|
| I | Introduce Topic | |
| O | Opinion Statement | |
| **Body Paragraph 1** |||
| R | Reason | |
| E | Evidence | |
| E | Elaboration | |
| C | Concluding Statement | |
| **Body Paragraph 2** |||
| R | Reason | |
| E | Evidence | |
| E | Elaboration | |
| C | Concluding Statement | |
| | | |
| O | Reinforce Opinion | |

## Part 2

| | |
|---|---|
| Does the introduction identify the text? | |
| Does the introduction identify the author? | |
| Does the introduction state the topic? | |
| Does the introduction provide an opinion and give two supporting reasons? | |

# Name

# Handout 34A: Focusing Question Task 3 Checklist

**Directions:** Use this checklist to revise your writing. Mark + for "yes" and Δ for "not yet." Ask someone (adult or peer) to evaluate your writing as well. Then answer the questions at the bottom of the page.

| Grade 3 Opinion Writing Checklist | Self +/ Δ | Peer +/ Δ | Teacher +/ Δ |
|---|---|---|---|
| **Structure** | | | |
| • I responded to all parts of the prompt. | | | |
| • I focused on my opinion. | | | |
| • I introduced the topic or text in my introductory paragraph. | | | |
| • I stated an opinion. | | | |
| • I organized or listed my reasons in a way that makes sense. | | | |
| • My concluding section refers to my opinion. | | | |
| • I used linking words and phrases to connect my opinion and reasons. | | | |
| **Development** | | | |
| • I supported my opinion with reasons related to how the art or text expresses a fact or important question about space. | | | |

| Style | | | |
|---|---|---|---|
| • I used simple, compound, and complex sentences. | | | |
| • I used vocabulary words that are appropriate to the topic. | | | |
| • I used and circled at least three new vocabulary words. | | | |
| • My writing is appropriate for the purpose and audience of the task. | | | |
| **Conventions** | | | |
| • I used pronouns for variety and flow. | | | |
| • I used coordinating and subordinating conjunctions that are appropriate to create compound and complex sentences. | | | |
| **Writing Process** | | | |
| • I used a Writing Planner to organize my ideas. | | | |
| • I provided thoughtful feedback in peer revision. | | | |
| • I used feedback in peer revision. | | | |
| **Total number of +'s:** | | | |

When you have finished reviewing your work, circle a pronoun in your essay. Use the space below to explain how the pronoun functions in the sentence.

Pronoun:

How does the pronoun function in the sentence?

# Name

# Handout 34B: Making Revisions

**Directions:** Read the paragraph below, and make revisions to meet the criteria on Handout 34A: Focusing Question Task 3 Checklist.

The class read many books about space in Module 2. The class learned a lot about space. One book the class read was *Moonshot*. *Moonshot* showed how exciting the trip to the moon was. The astronauts flew one hundred miles in twelve minutes. The astronauts traveled in a spaceship with no gravity. The astronauts were amazed by the moon. Neil Armstrong walked on the moon! The president called Neil Armstrong. Neil Armstrong looked at the earth from the surface of the moon. The astronauts returned to Earth.

# Name

# Handout 35A: Writing Planner

**Directions:** Use this graphic organizer to plan a response to the End-of-Module Task:

In your opinion, what is the most important thing people have done to learn about space?

| I | Introduce Topic | |
|---|---|---|
| O | Opinion Statement | |
| **Body Paragraph 1** |||
| R | Reason | |
| E | Evidence | |
| E | Elaboration | |
| C | Concluding Statement | |

|   |   | Body Paragraph 2 |
|---|---|---|
| R | Reason | |
| E | Evidence | |
| E | Elaboration | |
| C | Concluding Statement | |
| | | |
| O | Reinforce Opinion | |

## Part 2

| | |
|---|---|
| Does the introduction identify the text? | |
| Does the introduction identify the author? | |
| Does the introduction state the topic? | |
| Does the introduction provide an opinion and give two supporting reasons? | |

# Name

# Handout 36A: End-of-Module Task Checklist

**Directions:** Use this checklist to revise your writing. Mark + for "yes" and Δ for "not yet." Ask someone (adult or peer) to evaluate your writing as well.

|  | Self +/ Δ | Peer +/ Δ | Teacher +/ Δ |
|---|---|---|---|
| **Reading Comprehension** | | | |
| • I used textual evidence to support opinions. | | | |
| **Structure** | | | |
| • I responded to all parts of the prompt. | | | |
| • I focused on my opinion. | | | |
| • I introduced the topic or text in my introductory paragraph. | | | |
| • I stated an opinion. | | | |
| • I organized or listed my reasons in a way that makes sense. | | | |
| • My concluding section refers to my opinion. | | | |
| • I used linking words and phrases to connect my opinion and reasons. | | | |

| Development | | | |
|---|---|---|---|
| • I supported my opinion with reasons. | | | |
| **Style** | | | |
| • I used simple, compound, and complex sentences. | | | |
| • I used interesting adjectives and adverbs. | | | |
| • I used vocabulary words that are appropriate to the topic. | | | |
| • I used and circled at least three new vocabulary words. | | | |
| • My writing is appropriate for the purpose and audience of the task. | | | |
| **Conventions** | | | |
| • I used appropriate pronouns for variety and flow. | | | |
| • I used coordinating and subordinating conjunctions that are appropriate to create compound and complex sentences. | | | |
| **Writing Process** | | | |
| • I used a Writing Planner to organize my ideas. | | | |
| • I provided thoughtful feedback in peer revision. | | | |
| • I used feedback in peer revision. | | | |
| Total number of +'s: | | | |

# Name

# Volume of Reading Reflection Questions

**Text:** _____

**Author:** _____

**Topic:** _____

**Genre/Type of Book:** _____

Share your knowledge about outer space and space travel by responding to the questions below.

**Informational Text**

1. **Wonder:** What is one question about space you think this text will answer?

2. **Organize:** Pick one interesting topic the author presents about outer space. How is information about this topic organized for the reader to make it easier to understand?

3. **Reveal:** What is one claim about space or space travel that the author makes in this text? What evidence does the author give to support this claim?

4. **Distill:** Did the author have a favorable or unfavorable view of space? Provide evidence from the text to support your response.

5. **Know:** How does the information in this text compare to what you have already learned about outer space or space travel? Provide at least two examples of information that is the same and/or different.

6. **Vocabulary:** Write two important vocabulary words and definitions that you learned in this text into your Vocabulary Journal. What makes them important words to understand and know if you read about space or space travel?

## Literary Text

1. **Wonder:** What do you wonder after closely examining the front and back covers or after reading the first couple of pages of this text?

2. **Organize:** Write a short summary of the story including the character(s), setting, problem, and resolution.

3. **Reveal:** Does the story seem realistic to you? What elements of the story help to make it seem real?

4. **Distill:** What is the central message, lesson, or moral in this story? Provide evidence from the text to support your response.

5. **Know:** How has this story changed the way that you think about outer space, space travel, or astronauts?

6. **Vocabulary:** Write two important vocabulary words and definitions that you learned in this text into your Vocabulary Journal. What makes them important words to understand and know if you read about space or space travel?

# WIT & WISDOM FAMILY TIP SHEET

## WHAT IS MY THIRD GRADE STUDENT LEARNING IN MODULE 2?

Wit & Wisdom is our English curriculum. It builds knowledge of key topics in history, science, and literature through the study of excellent texts. By reading and responding to stories and nonfiction texts, we will build knowledge of the following topics:

Module 1: The Sea

**Module 2: Outer Space**

Module 3: A New Home

Module 4: Artists Make Art

In this second module, Outer Space, we will study how people have learned about space through history. By reading books and examining art, students explore our fascination with the cosmos, asking, How do people learn about space?

## OUR CLASS WILL READ THESE BOOKS:

### Picture Books (Informational)

- Moonshot: The Flight of Apollo 11, Brian Floca
- One Giant Leap, Robert Burleigh
- Starry Messenger: Galileo Galilei, Peter Sís

### Picture Book (Literary)

- Zathura, Chris Van Allsburg

### Articles

- "Galileo's Starry Night," Kelly Terwilliger
- "Greek Myths," American Museum of Natural History
- "Apollo 11: The Eagle Has Landed," Leigh Anderson

### Speech

"We Choose the Moon," from a speech by President John F. Kennedy

## Stories

- "Pegasus and Perseus," Anonymous
- "Pegasus and Bellerophon," Anonymous
- "Callisto and Her Son," Anonymous

## OUR CLASS WILL EXAMINE THESE WORKS OF ART:

- *Starfield*, Vija Celmins
- *Space Object Box: "Little Bear, etc." motif*, Joseph Cornell

## OUR CLASS WILL WATCH THESE VIDEOS:

- "Cronkite Anchors First Moon Walk," CBS
- "Moon 101," National Geographic

## OUR CLASS WILL ASK THESE QUESTIONS:

- How did Galileo learn about space?
- How did the astronauts of Apollo 11 learn about space?
- How do artists and writers help people learn about space?

## QUESTIONS TO ASK AT HOME

As you read with your third grade student, ask:

- *What's happening?*
- *What does a closer look at words and illustrations reveal about this text's deeper meaning?*

## BOOKS TO READ AT HOME

- *The Planet Gods: Myths and Facts About the Solar System*, Jacqueline Mitton
- *Once Upon a Starry Night: Book of Constellations*, Jacqueline Mitton
- *The Little Prince*, Antoine de Saint-Exupéry
- *The Moon*, Seymour Simon
- *Boy, Were We Wrong About the Solar System!*, Kathleen V. Kudlinski
- *Find the Constellations*, H. A. Rey
- *Next Time You See the Moon*, Emily Morgan
- *Reaching for the Moon*, Buzz Aldrin

- *Footprints on the Moon*, Alexandra Siy
- *Planets!*, TIME For Kids
- *Zoo in the Sky: A Book of Animal Constellations*, Jacqueline Mitton
- *Meteor!*, Patricia Polacco
- *The Moon Over Star*, Dianna Hutts Aston
- *Space*, Mary Pope Osborne and Will Osborne
- *Team Moon: How 400,000 People Landed Apollo 11 on the Moon*, Catherine Thimmesh
- *Moonwalk: The First Trip to the Moon*, Judy Donnelly
- *The Adventures of Tintin: Explorers on the Moon*, Hergé

## IDEAS FOR TALKING ABOUT SPACE

Go outside after dark together. Look up at the night sky, and ask:

- What do you notice and wonder about space?
- What constellations do you see?
- Would you travel to space if you could? Why or why not?

# CREDITS

Great Minds® has made every effort to obtain permission for the reprinting of all copyrighted material. If any owner of copyrighted material is not acknowledged herein, please contact Great Minds® for proper acknowledgment in all future editions and reprints of this module.

- All images are used under license from Shutterstock.com unless otherwise noted.

- Handouts 2A and 2D: "Galileo's Starry Night" by Kelly Terwilliger from Spider magazine, April 2010. Text copyright © 2010 by Carus Publishing Company. Reprinted by permission of Cricket Media. All Cricket Media material is copyrighted by Carus Publishing d/b/a Cricket Media, and/or various authors and illustrators. Any commercial use or distribution of material without permission is strictly prohibited. Please visit **http://www.cricketmedia.com/info/licensing2** for licensing and **http://www.cricketmedia.com** for subscriptions

- Assessment 8A: "Moon 101" transcript, National Geographic Creative

- Handout 18A: "Apollo 11: The Eagle Has Landed" by Leigh Anderson from Amazing Journeys, Appleseeds magazine, May/June 2009. Text copyright © 2009 by Carus Publishing Company. Reprinted by permission of Cricket Media. All Cricket Media material is copyrighted by Carus Publishing d/b/a Cricket Media, and/or various authors and illustrators. Any commercial use or distribution of material without permission is strictly prohibited. Please visit **http://www.cricketmedia.com/info/licensing2** for licensing and **http://www.cricketmedia.com** for subscriptions

- All material from the *Common Core State Standards for English Language Arts & Literacy in History/Social Studies, Science, and Technical Subjects* © Copyright 2010 National Governors Association Center for Best Practices and Council of Chief State School Officers. All rights reserved.

- For updated credit information, please visit **http://witeng.link/credits**.

## ACKNOWLEDGMENTS

### Great Minds® Staff

*The following writers, editors, reviewers, and support staff contributed to the development of this curriculum.*

Karen Aleo, Elizabeth Bailey, Ashley Bessicks, Sarah Brenner, Ann Brigham, Catherine Cafferty, Sheila Byrd-Carmichael, Lauren Chapalee, Emily Climer, Rebecca Cohen, Elaine Collins, Julia Dantchev, Beverly Davis, Shana Dinner de Vaca, Kristy Ellis, Moira Clarkin Evans, Marty Gephart, Mamie Goodson, Nora Graham, Lindsay Griffith, Lorraine Griffith, Christina Gonzalez, Emily Gula, Brenna Haffner, Joanna Hawkins, Elizabeth Haydel, Sarah Henchey, Trish Huerster, Ashley Hymel, Carol Jago, Mica Jochim, Jennifer Johnson, Mason Judy, Sara Judy, Lior Klirs, Shelly Knupp, Liana Krissoff, Sarah Kushner, Suzanne Lauchaire, Diana Leddy, David Liben, Farren Liben, Brittany Lowe, Whitney Lyle, Stephanie Kane-Mainier, Liz Manolis, Jennifer Marin, Audrey Mastroleo, Maya Marquez, Susannah Maynard, Cathy McGath, Emily McKean, Andrea Minich, Rebecca Moore, Lynne Munson, Carol Paiva, Michelle Palmieri, Tricia Parker, Marya Myers Parr, Meredith Phillips, Eden Plantz, Shilpa Raman, Rachel Rooney, Jennifer Ruppel, Julie Sawyer-Wood, Nicole Shivers, Danielle Shylit, Rachel Stack, Amelia Swabb, Vicki Taylor, Melissa Thomson, Lindsay Tomlinson, Tsianina Tovar, Sarah Turnage, Melissa Vail, Keenan Walsh, Michelle Warner, Julia Wasson, Katie Waters, Sarah Webb, Lynn Welch, Yvonne Guerrero Welch, Amy Wierzbicki, Margaret Wilson, Sarah Woodard, Lynn Woods, and Rachel Zindler

### Colleagues and Contributors

*We are grateful for the many educators, writers, and subject-matter experts who made this program possible.*

David Abel, Robin Agurkis, Sarah Ambrose, Rebeca Barroso, Julianne Barto, Amy Benjamin, Andrew Biemiller, Charlotte Boucher, Adam Cardais, Eric Carey, Jessica Carloni, Dawn Cavalieri, Janine Cody, Tequila Cornelious, David Cummings, Matt Davis, Thomas Easterling, Jeanette Edelstein, Sandra Engleman, Charles Fischer, Kath Gibbs, Natalie Goldstein, Laurie Gonsoulin, Dennis Hamel, Kristen Hayes, Steve Hettleman, Cara Hoppe, Libby Howard, Gail Kearns, Lisa King, Sarah Kopec, Andrew Krepp, Shannon Last, Ted MacInnis, Christina Martire, Alisha McCarthy, Cindy Medici, Brian Methe, Ivonne Mercado, Patricia Mickelberry, Jane Miller, Cathy Newton, Turi Nilsson, Julie Norris, Tara O'Hare, Galemarie Ola, Tamara Otto, Christine Palmtag, Dave Powers, Jeff Robinson, Karen Rollhauser, Tonya Romayne, Emmet Rosenfeld, Mike Russoniello, Deborah Samley, Casey Schultz, Renee Simpson, Rebecca Sklepovich, Kim Taylor, Tracy Vigliotti, Charmaine Whitman, Glenda Wisenburn-Burke, and Howard Yaffe

### Early Adopters

*The following early adopters provided invaluable insight and guidance for Wit & Wisdom:*

- Bourbonnais School District 53 • Bourbonnais, IL
- Coney Island Prep Middle School • Brooklyn, NY
- Gate City Charter School for the Arts • Merrimack, NH
- Hebrew Academy for Special Children • Brooklyn, NY
- Paris Independent Schools • Paris, KY
- Saydel Community School District • Saydel, IA
- Strive Collegiate Academy • Nashville, TN
- Valiente College Preparatory Charter School • South Gate, CA
- Voyageur Academy • Detroit, MI

Design Direction provided by Alton Creative, Inc.

Project management support, production design and copyediting services provided by ScribeConcepts.com

Copyediting services provided by Fine Lines Editing

Product management support provided by Sandhill Consulting